DATE DUE

D1507180

Also by Adele Scheele, Ph.D.
Published by Ballantine Books:

SKILLS FOR SUCCESS

MAKING COLLEGE PAY OFF

Adele Scheele, Ph.D.

BALLANTINE BOOKS • NEW YORK

Acknowledgments

The more I learn, the more I depend on the support, encouragement, and other demonstrations of faith from those people I enthusiastically work with and love—

Marilyn Abraham
Kenneth Barten
Virginia Faber
Elizabeth Franzeim
Jacqueline Hirtz
Susan Grode
D. Sam Scheele

Contents

Introduction: Some Tips on How to Choose a College

"I have never let my schooling interfere
with my education."
—Mark Twain

The purpose of education is to experiment, connect, set, and reset aims. Certainly these are the opportunities in life that the most successful achievers take. Why not learn them in the safest laboratory of life—college!

This book is about creating rich opportunities while you are in college or graduate school, about seeing college as a laboratory, replete with authorities, mentors, research programs, friends—a vital passage from theory to practice. It is, then, for anyone who is willing to look at school from a broader perspective, to see it as a microcosm of, and introduction to, the "real" world.

If you are not currently enrolled in a particular program, your first question is probably, "How should

I pick which college or graduate school to go to?" The easy answer is, "Pick the best." But what is "best" is not the same for each of us. Ultimately it matters less *where* you go to school than the amount of positive energy you put into it. Going to Harvard can help you get a better first job, there's no doubt about that. Having a Harvard M.B.A. or a Harvard law degree gives you a leading edge for hire by the most prestigious corporations, agencies, or firms *at first*. But there's no guarantee that your Harvard degree will keep you there. There is no guarantee that if you do not "use" Harvard, in the many senses that I mean "to use," as described in this book, that it will, in fact, offer you anything. It is a prestigious label, but that alone won't make you who you want to be.

Over the years as a career consultant, I have interviewed many people—both successful and not so successful—and I have learned that it isn't so much the specific college they attended but their willingness to devote themselves to achievement and to see and seize opportunity that accounted for their future success. Succeeding in college is the same as succeeding in any group—any family, any business. Regardless of the college, opportunity exists to do well if only you will recognize it and act on it. It takes intention and action, that mighty combination of will and deed, no matter where you are—junior high school, boarding school, small college, Ivy League university, multinational corporation or solo practice, vacation or retirement. A chance is always there—even in the everyday humdrum routine.

Often we don't believe it. We hold tenaciously to the idea that some force outside of ourselves can make us better. We fantasize that if only we could get into the best college or graduate school and into the best program with the best professor, we would have it made. Being able to recognize the fallacy of this kind of thinking will free us to examine more appropriate choices based on our needs and situation.

If you are wondering which school to attend, here is some food for thought. If you have already made that decision, chapter one begins on page 21.

Small Colleges

There are distinct advantages to small colleges. The first is what's called the "big fish, little pond" phenomenon. Being known among a few thousand students often makes even the shyest student able to compete. There is greater potential to develop leadership skills and participate in college activities in a more familylike and knowable population. Group support and expectation that you will participate is stronger, social life tends to be more closely knit, and relationships with college faculty and administration are often closer. In a small college it's easier for professors to get to know you, since they are more likely to be your classroom teachers. Not having research and the "publish-or-perish" dictum as their highest priority, professors are more likely to have the time and the inclination to care about what and how you learn. Your chances of attracting a professor's attention and even being directed toward one specialization or another are higher. The emphasis on education itself can be the primary focus of a college dedicated to academic excellence.

These very advantages can, of course, be disadvantages. Smallness can be a limitation. There can be less diversity of students and less variety of programs offered. Professors are less likely to be leading scholars and less likely to be engaged in the significant research typically carried on at larger universities or in graduate schools.

So how do you decide? The answer is that you have to figure out who you are and where you are in life to decide what you really need from school. If you need development and nurturing (and there's nothing wrong with that), then a small college could be a good starting point in your exploration. But if you are set firmly on your course, you might choose a large university for the generally high level of professional expertise and the quality of research facilities available.

Specialty Schools

Specialty schools—single sex, parochial, and technical colleges—offer even more clearly distinct advantages and disadvantages. Women from small women's colleges, for example, generally agree that the exclusion of men allows them a much greater potential for prominence in academic pursuits as well as the total freedom to strive and compete for leadership. They feel liberated from the powerful social constraint of holding themselves back—even unconsciously—to allow men to take the lead. Of course, to some, this exclusion of men is seen as a disadvantage, since it creates an unnatural environment in which to compete.

Parochial colleges offer the unique chance for students of similar values and beliefs to come to study together and form a double bond of faith and scholarship. Often these bonds last a lifetime. Learning from a faculty dedicated to teaching a curriculum under an umbrella of a common faith creates a very special, safe environment. Again, the disadvantages lie in the lack of diversity.

The advantage of technical colleges lies in their focus on a single career, whether it is art or engineering. A spirit of camaraderie among the students is enhanced by a sense of a shared vocational "mission." Professors assume the role of coaches to recognize your special talents and point you in new directions. Again, the disadvantage is the lack of diversity, especially in terms of the limited curriculum. For instance, an art school usually lacks a program of sciences; a science school usually lacks an arts program. And that doesn't mean just classes, but all the extracurricular activity that surrounds any program, from exhibits and performances to special seminars and visits to campus from professionals in a given field. The atmosphere of intellectual curiosity and exploration over a wide range of subjects is often missing in these colleges. Students are fairly well tracked in the discipline of their choice and are eager to pursue it and get on with their professional lives. This is not to say that there is no intellectual or artistic curiosity among people who pursue professions, but among these students you will find greater goal-orientation than you might encounter at a more diverse, exploratory university.

Community Colleges

Community colleges offer two kinds of programs: the complete two-year program at the end of which you receive a degree; and the two-year transfer program designed to segue into a four-year program. Both meet two specific needs of many students—financial and academic. If you cannot afford the tuition of a four-year college, you can take full advantage of the practically free community colleges. You can work part-time to save up for tuition for your last two years at a four-year college. Also, if your high school grades were not high enough, you can attend a community college until you pull up your average.

Community colleges offer a diverse faculty. Teachers are often young, former high school teachers who are in the process of getting their doctorate degrees. Often they can provide a closer, more sensitive relationship with students.

Universities

Most universities operate like small cities in the size and scope of their activities. With student populations approximating 25,000, the dilemma here is in knowing even a handful of classmates and choosing which program to participate in. Still, small communities of students form around special interests. As a general rule, the larger the institution is, the greater the sophistication and range of programs offered. But the competition is more intense, both academically and socially. So, while there is much greater competition for positions in student government, for example, there is also much more opportunity to participate in other areas of interest, say, in a world affairs council, a radical journal, or a very specialized scientific research association.

Faculty members are chosen for their excellent professional reputations, which are built upon research. Considered experts in their field, they often, however, are much more enthusiastic about their particular subject matter than they are about teaching students. This means that teaching assistants, graduate students themselves, are more likely to be your classroom instructors than the famous professor you had hoped for, but the excitement and the inspiration that comes from state-of-the-art research conducted right at the very moment can make up for that. The availability of large grants and alumni support also provides a tremendous range of resources (e.g., libraries, theaters, exhibits) that are either free or inexpensive to students, and cannot be matched on any other kind of campus.

On the negative side, the sheer size of a university can create a concomitant aloofness. It is, therefore, up to each student to pursue an academic program with activities that are involving in order not to lose individuality.

Home or Away

Most young people experience the need to break away from the dependency of home life, and in that light, living on campus or at least on your own is preferable to living at home while going to college. College represents, for most students, the first time that they develop a sense of their own individuality and maturity, separate from family. It is often the first time students discipline themselves, both academically and socially, and are responsible for their own money. Every successful person whom I have interviewed underscores this need for independence from family, even if you have to work part-time to afford it. If you live in or near the city your college is in, and unless money is an insurmountable problem, consider renting a room in a boarding house or sharing an apartment with others a short distance from your family. Obviously it is possible to go to a university or a college in town while living at home, but all transitions become harder as families used to living in the foreground must be relegated to the background.

Urban vs. Rural

Making the choice between going to an educational institution in the middle of a metropolitan area or one in a rural setting can be perplexing. Colleges in urban locations offer access to arts and sciences plus business and service communities. Besides the stimulation this affords, this link provides greater opportunity for forming valuable contacts. Rural colleges or universities, on the other hand, are much like company towns in that they are the sole central purpose of the town. The university becomes a macrocosm. The town and university are united; students and professors participate in daily life and are therefore freer to mingle together. This closeness is especially important to many students.

Evaluations

After deciding what you want from a school and making a preliminary list of which schools meet your needs, you can start an active exploration period as early as one year before you apply. All colleges are rated and their departments analyzed. These ratings and analyses, ranking the best colleges and universities in general and their departments in particular, are available in guides published by Barron's, Peterson's, and *The New York Times*, as well as in various professional journals. Most professions, such as education, science, the arts, publish one or more journals which annually rate the best colleges and universities in the field. The *Chronicle of Higher Education*, which is available in every college library, regularly rates the various departments of a university. You owe it to yourself to consider an institution where your chosen discipline is rated highly and to know which professors are where.

Visit several colleges and universities during a regular session, not during breaks. Select both an urban and a rural university if you can't make up your mind between them. Or a small and a large campus. See for yourself. You can plan a trip with your family or friends; you don't have to go alone. At first, I would recommend just "hanging out" at the student union, the library, the gym, or the bookstore to pick up clues. Talk to students and ask them what they like and don't like about their school. From a class catalog, find out the schedule of classes in your field of interest. If the class is large, you can sit in and see for yourself the kind of instruction going on. If the class is small, and you will be noticed, introduce yourself to the professor, explain your interests, and you will probably be invited in. Do not be afraid of stopping by to visit a few instructors and professors. Explain that you are considering attending their college or university. Tell some of your interests and, for openers, ask if they think someone with your background and interests might do well there. Then ask something about their area. Some professors will be willing to take the time to answer you, whereas obviously others will not. If none of them will talk to you, that's a clue in itself.

Find alumni in your area, if you can, and ask if they would choose the same college if they had it to do over again. If you know people who are active in your chosen field, ask their advice on undergraduate or graduate schools. Take your time making your decision.

But remember, even if you do not get into the

college or university of your choice, even if, because of proximity or any other specific constraint, your final choice is not your ideal wish, there is more to life than the label of the college from which you graduate. Your essential mission in college is to develop yourself, to learn, to find ways to create opportunities.

Our aims in college are threefold: (1) learning: the accumulation of knowledge for its own sake; (2) specific preparation for a career; and (3) the development of self-discipline and courage. College is a time of preparation for life. The skills that I'm going to discuss in this book work in every single college setting, small or large, co-ed or single sex, town or country, Ivy League or technical.

1

The "Good Student" Trap

"I try to act as if I make a difference."
—William James

College is an experiment in hope. It's also a risky investment for us all. Whether it is graduate or undergraduate school, a two-year program or an eight-year program, we entrust time in our lives to school for both a new identity and a ticket to the outside world. We come to college with unspoken anticipation of all that will be done for us. We expect to be made acceptable, valuable, and finally employable in the eyes of the world. We also hope that magic answers will be revealed to us through academic study, leading us to guaranteed success in the outside world. By graduation or completion of our chosen program, we presume everything will be dazzlingly clear; we will be made brilliant, and all knowledge will be accessible to us. Of course we never admit this aloud; seldom is it conscious. But deep down, we believe it will happen.

I've counseled and been a consultant to countless people who all had faith in this magic—many of whom were disappointed when the expected alchemy never took place. They discovered, years later, that this powerful, magical process just doesn't "happen." *You make it happen.* You can believe in magic, but *you* must be the magician.

We have all been conditioned to wait for things to happen to us, instead of making things happen. If you think you have escaped this conditioning, then think again—back to your previous schooling. Most of us learned that we would excel, or at least pass, if we did the work assigned to us by our teachers. And that's exactly what occurred. We would find out whether a certain test covered all of chapter five, or only a part of it, whether the assigned paper was to be ten pages long or thirty. Even "extra credit" was determined for us: two book reports by the same author. Remember? We learned to: (1) find out what was expected of us, (2) do it, and (3) wait for a response. And we were always responded to specifically in the form of a grade. When all our grades were assembled and averaged, we were passed. After we took all the required courses, we were promoted—from fifth grade to sixth grade, from sophomore to junior, from first year of law school to second. But what did we really learn? *System Dependency!* How? We learned the dogma of absolute truth—right answers and wrong ones. We learned that you get one shot at a test or a paper and that's it; that your grades were averaged and weighed and that a number was everything. We learned that the person who knew the greatest number of right answers was rewarded by being the first in his or her class, vale-dictorian or member of the law review.

Nothing like this happens in real life. Yet too many of us never recognize it. We are the same passive students at ten or twenty-five or forty-four as we were at fourteen, continuing the teacher-student dichotomy, which we automatically transfer to the employer-employee relationship. And we found that though studying history or art or anthropology might have been interesting, it alone didn't lead to much else—like new experiences, contacts, or even a job. Much disappointment has resulted from this "mis-use" of college. It's time to retrain ourselves to ap-proach school in the same positive, productive, active way that successful people approach life.

If you follow the suggestions and advice set forth in this book, college will become all that you wished for—a time for learning, for broadening horizons, a time to discover who you are and how you work with others, for setting goals and making things happen. In short, college is a time for developing skills that will serve you far beyond your college years, which, even more than your degree, will prepare you for entrance into the "real" world.

Sustainers vs. Achievers

First let's look at what successful people do. As a career specialist, I've consulted, coached, and interviewed people—from teachers to banking executives—who want to be, or already are, successful at what they do. From mapping their lives, I have discovered that people who are successful in work have also been successful in certain aspects of their schooling. I have also found that people in every endeavor fall into one of two general patterns of behavior. At one end of the spectrum are the Achievers—the successful people. We all know who they are. I don't call those at the opposite end failures. Rather I call them Sustainers. They're not really failing at what they do, but they're not making anything happen for themselves either. They are simply sustaining.

Sometimes Sustainers and Achievers are actually two different kinds of people, but mostly each of us slides from passive to active mode during the course of a day, an hour, or a year. My goal is to make you an Achiever and to motivate you to achieve in every way while you're in college, and with those same skills go on to be successful in life.

Sustainers act in life as they did in school. In fact they fall into the Good Student Syndrome. "Good" here means passively waiting for grades, and doing little beyond that. They do their jobs well, even excellently, and then wait first for their teachers and later their bosses to praise their work and promote them.

But waiting is never recognized by those in position above you. People who sit and wait do not contribute. And no boss wants to promote someone who doesn't have something to offer the management team. Neither would you. Doing the job well (i.e., getting good grades) by itself does not get you promoted in the real world. You have to do *more* than your share. In the real world, the work world, Sustainers tend to grow invisible. Not understanding their lack of recognition, they grumble and gripe about their superiors and their achieving peers who move rapidly above them. They are unhappy with the entire company, and they often let those around them know it!

Achievers act differently. To be sure, they do their jobs well, but that's where the resemblance to Sustainers ends. Achievers do more than their work requires; they generate ideas, and work long hours. But beyond that, Achievers know the value of positive self-presentation in order to get the recognition they deserve. They are open to new situations and experiences. They understand the importance of

27

forming connections and alliances that result in the healthy exchange of ideas and sharing of experiences that are vital in the marketplace.

Getting Recognition

Look again at school and see what it teaches implicitly: One professor leads a class of any number of students, creating a horizontal power structure in which many people, equal in nonpower status, look toward one ultimate authority. How then do students get attention and recognition? Achievers learn to get the desired attention by doing excellent work combined with gaining favor. Some others learn to gain attention by poor disciplinary behavior. But the great majority of us are overlooked—and do nothing about it. If you are thinking that it is a silly or unimportant point, think back to your earliest days of school.

Do you recall what most of us did when we were back, say, in junior high school? If we didn't get the recognition we wanted from our teachers, we turned to each other for peer group approval. The group became the most powerful determiner of our actions and in turn set the standards by which we defined ourselves. Whether our groups or cliques were based on what our fathers did or made, how we dressed, our race, sex, religion, or class, athletic prowess or personal attractiveness, we conformed to the standards of the group, rarely daring to explore beyond its self-limiting boundaries. And this is the model we carry into our working lives—adapting to a peer group for inclusion, initially, and then conforming to stay in.

Just as seventh graders eat lunch with only other seventh graders, or college seniors with other college seniors, adult men and women who are Sustainers continue to look to each other in their peer level for approval instead of others on different levels, especially higher-ups in their organizations. Real life—the work world—is multidimensional and completely unlike the horizontal power structure of school. Some of us work alone or in partnership, but most of us work in large organizations based on a pyramid structure. There is one top position followed by decreasing levels of authority that contain an increasing number of people responsible for numerous divisions and departments. If you want more—new challenges, responsibilities, and rewards—ask yourself who believes in you and who has the power to promote you. Your peers and colleagues can't; they simply don't have the authority. Only your superiors can. You must get their attention, get them to know who you are and recognize your worth. In the seventh grade, you wouldn't try to get the attention of your teachers for fear of being labeled a brown-noser. But life isn't seventh grade fortunately; it's not that simple or terrible. So instead of thinking of college as a more difficult seventh grade, learn to use college like the real world. Step up and out of the suffocating Sustainer's box and stop pulling the lid tighter down on your own possibilities. Remember, the longer you sit and wait, the harder it is to move up. The passive "good student" attitude that turns adults into Sustainers absolutely stifles any chance for people to become motivated, impassioned, or connected to new ideas and networks of people. Don't be afraid to make that extra effort. Doing only the minimum requirement is the grossest misunderstanding of what college is all about!

Practice Experimenting

The need to perform well and get good grades is an essential part of going to school. Good grades got you into college in the first place, and high academic performance is a good indicator to future employers of your ability to do well in a job. Unfortunately, the standard for measuring performance in college is the test. Nobody likes taking tests. They create anxiety, are not always fair, and do not always seem to measure accurately what you know about your subject. But until someone comes up with a better system, we have to live with them. The danger in this emphasis on taking tests and making the grade is that we come to think of all life situations in terms of pass or fail. This conditioning gives us a heightened fear of failure, that, as adults, often inhibits us from *doing*. But there are no such absolutes in life. What we have to do is give up thinking that school is only a test. Test-taking is not fun and essentially presents little real challenge to learning about process and change.

For what reason do we strive to do well in tests? Only to get a grade. If you doubt me, just look at what happens: Most of us are highly anxious before and during the test. If our grade is bad, most of us doubt ourselves, even see ourselves as failures. In school, we almost never get the chance to turn a C into an A in a second attempt. If our grade is good, we breathe a sigh of relief, then get ready for the next test. Ironically, some good students fear failure so much that no matter how well they perform they really believe that they have failed until the grades are posted and they discover that they did exceptionally well. Students develop a fear of being tested in any situation. The trick is learning how to get beyond this phobia, just as all Achievers have learned to transcend their fear of failure. Achievers have come to consider life or school as an experiment instead of only a test. Does this sound Pollyannaish? Maybe, but it works.

Let's look at the process of a scientific experiment. First, you develop your hypothesis; then you test it. If it works, you feel pleased because you've proved your theory. Being right certainly feels good. But have you learned anything? No, you already knew it; only now you are more sure and can tell others. But suppose you don't prove what you set out to at first. You feel terrible about not being right. In fact, you were wrong. But have you failed? Only if you think the experiment is a test. If so, then by getting the "wrong answer" you have failed. You could decide to quit then and there. If, however, you go on in true experimental fashion, restructuring your hypothesis, reexamining your variables, trying another approach, applying your own educated hunches, only then do you discover things you didn't know before. You increase your store of knowledge until you finally hit upon the correct hypothesis. It's more like that old adage that grew from generations of collected wisdom: "If at first you don't succeed, try, try again." The critical phrase must have been omitted—"another way, each time."

What is stopping you from thinking of college (graduate or undergraduate) as an experiment instead of a test? An experiment to find out what you like to study, whom you like to study with, and who you would like to become? Don't turn college into one large test with many small tests along the way. The college experience is much broader than that. You will simply be passing: passing tests, passing time, passing by a greater college experience, passing up possibilities for achievement, passing through life; becoming a Sustainer.

Decide. The rest of this book is only for those of you interested in achieving and being an experimenter. College can be a period of time out from the real world, or it can be a head start into the real world. It's what *you* make it.

Susan was a high achiever in high school. A 3.8 grade average got her into UCLA where she studied her favorite language—French. She did well, got almost all A's, and graduated near the top of her class with a B.A. in French. She did little else except play tennis on Sundays and waitress at night at a local coffee shop. Susan figured that armed with a degree and proficiency in a foreign language, a job—she hoped in Paris, the city of her dreams—would be hers upon graduation.

Near the end of her last semester Susan developed what she called "graduationitis" (a student disease common to both Achievers and Sustainers). After writing scores of letters requesting job information Susan realized that she was not equipped with attractive qualifications. No one seemed interested in even answering her queries, let alone employing her. What could she do with a B.A. in French? There were many people around who were fluent in French, and they were teachers with at least a master's degree. But Susan didn't want to teach or go to graduate school. As for getting employment overseas with an American company, Susan discovered that such jobs were plums given as a reward to company men or women who put in time, energy, and developed a necessary skill, like marketing, that went beyond the ability to speak French. So that hope was dashed. Another alternative was joining the military overseas, but that had little appeal for Susan. Susan suddenly felt that college had been a complete waste; she felt victimized, duped, and fell into a profound state of depression.

From my viewpoint, however, no experience is ever wasted. After all, the study of another language and culture does provide a valuable framework. But by not "using" college, Susan certainly did waste all kinds of valuable opportunities. She could have made friends with her French professors and met their friends, or studied the French import business, volunteered time to the French consulate, or translated for the mayor's office. She might even have worked part-time at a French bank. Susan certainly could have waitressed at a French restaurant rather than a coffee shop, connecting herself to a chef or owner, even French customers. She could have developed her leadership abilities by joining the French club and becoming an officer or inviting French artists, politicians, and business people to campus for a special seminar or colloquium. She could have even spent her junior year in France, working part-time for an American company with offices in Paris.

Pursuing these extracurriculars would have taken time, courage, research, and energy. But all these avenues of exploration would have taught Susan something and would have been fun in the process. Even if her grade point had dropped, she would have gained building blocks to her future, even a passport to Paris.

You can be active in a place where you've been conditioned to be passive. You can use test taking as an activity to stimulate the other areas of your life so that your goals have a chance of being fulfilled, making way for you to create new goals. It is my goal to make you experience college as an experimental laboratory—not a self-contained ivory tower, but a source of people, contacts, minds, power, creativity, and opportunity—and to show you that it is as open-ended as you are open-minded and willing to risk, share, and explore all that college has to offer.

2

Mentors: Making the Most of Student-Professor Relationships

"Life is not complete until you acquire a master."
—Shri Satyapal Ji

Learning the Dynamics

Relationships are tricky things. No getting around that. The dynamics of relationships between friends and lovers has been the subject of countless books. The relationship between student and professor is unique and complicated by its inequality. The only real model we have for it is the relationship of child to parent. The child-parent relationship is one of near total dependency. On the one hand, parents expect that children will be self-indulgent, rebellious, complaining, boring, demanding, nonsupportive, and blaming. On the other hand, they want them to be obedient, achieving, grateful, and loving. The role of parent is that of nurturer and caretaker. Parents provide their children with a home and financial support, and through discipline, guidance, and love prepare them for eventual independence.

As students we must learn to separate the student role from the role of the child. Blind obedience, total dependency, tough rebelliousness, or feigned indifference are all inappropriate ways of relating to your professors. Nevertheless, if you look around your class or seminar, I'd bet you'd see examples of this kind of behavior. Don't make the same mistakes. Better models for interaction exist.

The relationship of apprentice to master is closer to what a healthy and productive student-professor relationship should be. In this model from the pre-industrial era, the young apprentice became an indentured servant to a master artist or craftsman for a certain period of time in order to learn his master's trade. Performing menial tasks at first, the apprentice slowly learned his craft until he was able to take over for the master or set out on his own. The same system can work in college. Here, the professor becomes the master and the student, the apprentice. I am suggesting that you can establish such a relationship with a professor in a specific discipline. I have studied such relationships and seen them lead to great achievements.

Building the Relationship

It is important to find professors whose ideas and research are respected within their field. You want professors to be not only interesting or entertaining but well connected. If you don't know whom to consider, and it's often difficult to know, ask around. Or go to the library and find the *citations index*, which lists who has cited any given professor's work, how many times, in which publications, and when. An often-cited professor is a well-connected one!

Once you find a professor whom you respect, it is then up to you to initiate the relationship. The best first step is simple conversation. Ask your professor for advice or support on a specific problem, ask him to elaborate on an anecdote he told in class, or try to spend time in the departmental office. You can usually do any of the following: Take as many of his courses as possible; read his published papers and books; initiate discussions on the topic during office hours, or talk informally after class. In short, demonstrate your interest in him!

Most successful people I have interviewed told me that they had several mentors who were critical to their development. In fact, different mentors had been helpful during different stages of career development. These mentors showed them the ropes, introduced them to other people, and advised them on all levels of decisions and strategies. Students, therefore, can also think of having several professors with whom they are close in order to begin this process of transference of knowledge and values. Mentors are really like coaches. They can show you how to build on what you have learned and how to apply it in new directions.

Let's see how this mentor system works. A top-notch computer analyst told me that his entire career had actually been formed because of an impressive, charismatic, brilliant professor. As a student, he openly demonstrated his awe, coming to class early and staying late to discuss the problems that he had been working on. During the course of a year he developed a close relationship with his professor, who encouraged him to change his field from industrial engineering to economics. The professor introduced him to a prominent graduate professor and paved the way for a fellowship and advanced study, which he couldn't have gotten or even thought of by himself. Now the professor didn't single this student out from hundreds of others just because he was good. There are, after all, many good students. The reason that this particular student was propelled in this way was largely due to the effort the student had originally made to become close to a professor.

It is also true that these relationships are mutually beneficial. You may not think that you contribute to this relationship, but you do. It's easy to see the benefit to the student, but what about the professor? Let's look at the two worlds they live in. The first is the theoretical world of research. "Publish or Perish" is the law, and professors' tenure, success, and salary rests on their reputation as significant thinkers, which, in turn, are attested to by their ability to attract grants and contracts. These grants and contracts are a major source of financial support for the university. Student tuition, in fact, contributes only a small percentage to the operating costs of any university. In a strict economic sense, the student is relatively unimportant. For this reason teaching ability is often less critical than grant-getting ability in professors' careers. They are under tremendous pressure to conduct research and to publish in order to maintain their reputations and ensure their ability to be awarded grants.

Most professors have their work published in academic journals, where it is usually reviewed by colleagues. Most of the reviews are highly critical rather than laudatory. Yet professors, like all other humans, need as much validation and support as they can get. Providing your professor-mentor with sincere praise and admiration is your role on this two-way street.

The professor's second world is political. It encompasses responsibilities on academic committees and within university associations as well as administrative duties within a department. These tasks are time-consuming and usually obligatory. Who then provides the necessary positive feedback that professors need to carry on? You do, as vitally interested, gifted, willing students. Recognizing that this relationship is reciprocal actually enables each side to give even more.

Let's look at another example of a successful student-professor relationship. Ann was studying art history when a family problem arose that would have cost her an entire college education had it not been for the intervention of one of her professors. Ann's father fell ill and lost his job. The family was strapped, unable to make its mortgage payments, let alone meet the daughter's tuition. Ann panicked and was ready to quit her expensive Ivy League school and find a full-time job to support her family. One of her art professors, with whom she had already developed a strong rapport, rescued her. He convinced her to stay on by helping her get a fifty percent scholarship and a part-time job at night as a guard. The job allowed her some time to study—a perfect arrangement. The continuous moral support that her professor provided was also vital to Ann's college career—which turned out to be extraordinary—honors, grants, and two articles coauthored with her mentor. She was on her way in a highly competitive field.

Finding a professor-mentor is often harder when older people are students. Being the same age as one's professor can be initially uncomfortable for both sides. Returning students can make two basic errors —overplaying or underplaying their role. Older students often feel more colleaguelike, but they still have to seek advice and guidance without making the mistake of falling back to a completely subservient student role. Sometimes they regress from age thirty or forty to become an eighteen-year-old, acting as if they were a blank slate to be drawn on by the other. It is not unusual to regress to the age when they were in school, much like divorced people, who, single again at forty, suddenly find themselves dating with the same fears they had when they were eighteen. By being aware that this can happen, they can overcome these illusions in order to act appropriately.

Older students are often tempted to dazzle their professors with their own prior successful experiences, and unintentionally create a threatening, even competitive, situation. Roberta, at thirty-eight, had come back to college to study psychology at the graduate level after she had already administered a mental health clinic. She claimed that her hardest adjustment to college lay in not being offended by some of the simplistic or redundant ideas her professors presented to students who had never even seen a mental health environment. Her professor never ran such a clinic, but did have the experience of theoretical research on his side. Imagine Roberta's holding forth in a debate or constantly trying to have the last word in class. She had to abandon her need to prove herself right and find an appropriate balance so that her professors could acknowledge her experience and still accept her admiration of them. She had to learn a new diplomacy; otherwise she would have broadcast the message: "I know it all already. I'm just taking this course because it's required. You can't teach me anything."

How could Roberta have best benefited from her experiences? She might have brought up situations in which the mental health clinic staff were stuck with a problem and ask how they might have handled the situation better. Or she could have reflected about her unique experiences as administrator observing psychologists and psychiatrists working with certain groups of people with whom they had either successes or failures. Or, she might have suggested a pilot research program to train administrators to be counselors because their proximity had led to so much direct observation with behavioral patterns and interactions.

Another example of a successful mentor-student relationship can be seen in the story of Claude, a graduate student in sociology who became a research assistant to a top grant-getting professor at a prestigious state university. From performing a relatively insignificant task in one area of data collections, Claude saw where he could contribute more than the job required by coordinating the schedules and charting the progress of all the other data-collecting student researchers. By developing a specialized role for himself, Claude soon became counted on. He enrolled in all of the professor's courses over the following two years so he could watch him work and learn more about how he thought. Claude often visited him during office hours and asked him about his research and gradually read it all. In return, he was greatly rewarded. Not just in raises and a full scholarship, though that was, of course, tremendously helpful. But he was also given a special grant plus a portion of the study to conduct as his master's thesis, which in turn provided him with an impressive doctoral program. More than getting a scholarship and research project, Claude had the rich opportunity to watch a successful professor work in academia, including the writing and getting of grants, the implementation of major research, the reciprocity among other professionals in that university and others across the country. Claude was also privy to the way the professor acted politically in his voluntary-but-necessary major committees of tenure and development. He witnessed his successful style of decision making. Then when he was ready to apply for a doctoral program, his mentor personally referred him to a team of world-famous professors who had even more connections to offer. The sponsorship of Claude's first professor launched Claude's growth in his field. No student with only straight A's could have gained so much.

Do you think that what Claude did to get his initial job was worth the risk? What risk? you may ask. Claude chanced being called a brown-noser at least by some cynics in his class. Not only did Claude survive any name calling, but he succeeded far beyond any of his disdaining peers. They righteously refused to "use" their professors, and that refusal cost them their professional lives. At the end of the term, the nonconnected good-student Sustainers had grades to be proud of but no references, no exposure to new people who could open doors, and no new insights beyond their rigorously studied discipline. The cynics were actually hurt by their beliefs that school is only for passing tests and getting grades. It is they who misuse a system when they fail to recognize their part in a human enterprise.

Risk forming a relationship with one or more of your professors. It might be uncomfortable, even frightening to initiate, but that's true for all new and worthwhile pursuits. In actuality, the risk is so minimal. Be fair to yourself; you are not stupid or you wouldn't be in college in the first place. Wanting to learn more is the reason you're in school. You need to confront your own fears. One of the traits that separates the Sustainers from the Achievers is that the Achievers move even when they are afraid, whereas the Sustainers stop themselves with their fear. Mark Twain said it well, "Courage is not the absence of fear, but the mastery of it."

A word of caution may be necessary here. Too much of a good thing is not good. Turning a professor into a god who has all the answers is not productive—it precludes the meaningful exchange of ideas. Attaching yourself to a professor-mentor you respect for his or her intelligence and knowledge is not the same as hero worship. But, it is possible that you will become entranced by a seemingly ideal professor. If this happens, don't worry. It's a natural reaction and a phase to be lived through. Like the apprentice, as you gain knowledge and develop your expertise, you will eventually stand next to your professor as an equal. These are the phases of our growth, from which we shouldn't shy away.

Significant Others

Professors are not the only people on campus worthy of forming relationships with. For example, speakers who visit a campus can be approached by simply introducing yourself after their lecture. Later you'll be able to follow through with a letter which can open with "We met at…" It's also good business to have a friendly relationship with your advisor and department head and their staff. And don't exclude university administrative assistants who are responsible for student records, grants, and similar functions. These people can be tremendously helpful to you in ways that your professors, whose expertise is usually confined to their areas of study, cannot be. For example, if you are requesting special permission to take a course not usually open to you, or you need to petition to receive credit for a past course, talk to an administrator or assistant. They usually know all the rules of the game and can show you the best way to present your case. They often know about the availability of fellowships, grants, and other benefits. Think of these people as friends. They are there to help you. Don't wait until you're in the middle of a crisis to pay them a visit! It makes sense that when you need their help, they will be more responsive to you if they already know who you are. It's human nature.

3

The Double Agenda: Making the Most of Tests and Papers

"Talent is what you possess. Genius is
what possesses you."
—Malcolm Cowley

In early primitive societies, young men were initiated by ferocious trial before assuming their places as men in the tribe. These tests were arduous and life risking; only the brave and strong lived through them. What was being tested was courage and motivation as much as physical prowess.

Although different in form, we have the same concept of rites of passage—proof positive that our young and inexperienced are ready to take their place in society. Sometimes delayed, and certainly not life threatening, our modern rites are academic. We prove ourselves in school through the writing of papers—from short pieces to theses and dissertations—and the taking of written and oral examinations. These are proof of our ability to survive not physically but mentally. Papers and exams have become demonstrations to our professors that we can think, analyze, research, understand, and connect with our heritage, and, it is hoped, contribute fresh and useful ideas—in short, assume our places in the world as responsible adults. But in addition to getting us a grade and getting us by in a given course, does this test-taking or paper-writing process really give us any skills we can build on? What about preparation for later life? Can we ever be free of performing within a given framework? Think of it that way. Since tests are mandatory and since papers are assigned and you have to produce something anyway, you might as well work toward your own best advantage. Make the most possible use of your time—establish your own "double agenda"!

Papers

Papers, whether short or long, present an opportunity to develop your double agenda. First, you must meet the requirements set by the professor for the course. Second, you want to meet your own needs and goals. If you don't recognize what they are immediately, ask yourself what you wish would happen by the end of this course or general program. This allows you to sow the seeds for opportunity from what could have been just an obligatory classroom assignment. You learn to use school to its utmost advantage by making a name for yourself and creating a place for yourself within the system. Here are several ways to start.

A good source of material is your professor's current topic of research. Ask what he or she needs help with or wants to do next. This may sound intimidating, but remember, professors can always use help; rarely do they have an adequate staff of researchers. Begin by talking over the subject area with your professor. Sometimes together you will hit upon a spin-off topic that neither of you would have thought of before. Perhaps you can expand upon an idea in one of his or her papers. The very act of discussing your work directly builds up the relationship you've started with your professor in powerful and concrete ways.

The idea of building onto or jumping off from a professor's work is especially viable for graduate students who need material for theses and dissertations. But there is no rule against undergraduates doing it too. In fact, it would be a great spur to any undergraduate who intends to continue in a field. Every professor whom I have spoken to agrees, and has been instrumental in guiding interested undergraduates and helping them plan and prepare for graduate programs. All it takes from you is the willingness to take the first step.

Another, perhaps more challenging, alternative, is to develop your own specialization that you would like to pursue over the long run. Pick a topic in your field of study, something you are really interested in and want to explore further. That topic can become the theme of all your course work, and you can develop different facets in every course requiring a paper. That way you develop expertise and actually become involved in an area that is compelling *to you!*

If, for example, you are an education major but think that you would rather work in a business organization than teach, you might want to consider designing training aids or developing management training programs. Therefore, in papers for your major or other classes, you might want to: (1) research the history and success rates of specific aids; (2) compare the product differences and similarities among diverse industries; (3) volunteer to work, whether you'll be paid or not, on an actual design project; and (4) take electives in related fields—art design, computer design, communication theory, or management courses in training. Thus, your course work and related activities enable you to develop various aspects of your specialty.

Let me show you a case in point. Tired of graduate school and eager to get out to work, a psychology student had to face writing a thesis. Instead of picking a subject that interested him, one that related to the work he wanted to do, he chose a simple topic he thought would easily satisfy his professor. Then he undertook the usual laborious task of programming data—data, in this case, that he didn't care about in the first place and had to spend endless tedious hours analyzing. The result was predictable. He wrote a slipshod first draft that was turned down by his professor. He put off doing the final draft because he was so bored. He is now a good candidate for that all-too-common degree, the A.B.D. (All But Dissertation). He'll need a lot of motivation to get going again, if indeed, he can. I call that waste, complete waste. Find something that pulls you, interests you, turns you on, and do it. If there is nothing like that immediately, wait and search for it. College is a time of personal direction-finding too.

That's fine, you say, for dissertations or masters theses, but what can I do in regular undergraduate or even graduate courses? Let's say that you're interested in business as a possibility for a career choice, but you're not sure. Right now you're taking several art courses because you like art but you're not sure how art and business mix. Why not interview artists who live in your area to find out how they sell their work. Or, you might do a paper on art patrons, which will give you the opportunity to seek out new people outside the university. Later, when you graduate and are looking for a place to begin working, the people you have met might be able to help you, if not employ you themselves.

Another payoff is the possibility of publishing your paper. Any paper you write for a professor takes time and effort, so why not put in a little extra effort and make it count doubly? Write it with an eye for publication in a professional magazine, journal, or newspaper. In California, a political science undergraduate who was studying the situation in the Middle East came up with an unusual solution for one aspect of the tyrannous political strife and sent her theory to the *Christian Science Monitor*'s Op Ed page (the page opposite the editorials saved for opinions from the community). The paper printed it. This boosted her status on campus, but even more rewarding than that, a professor at a prestigious eastern university read it and was impressed with her fresh ideas. He offered her a fellowship to study with him in a special master's program; she, of course, accepted enthusiastically. By the simple act of sending her paper to the newspaper, she set off a chain of events that could not have happened if she had been merely content to sit back and get an A.

Projects

Every course has its requirements. Often you are
able to substitute a special project for the usual exam.
Projects offer all kinds of possibilities for you to explore interests and develop connections to the outside world. For example, if you are enrolled in
business or management school, you can design sur-
veys that you can then use to contact the marketing,
advertising, operations, or personnel departments of
corporations, whatever area interests you most. Your
survey can cover such subjects as the changing philosophy of employment, comparative studies in pro-
ductivity, new technologies and resulting new
products, or the training of new workers. Interviewing managers or employees whom they select to help
you with your study and then sharing the results

with them lets them get to know you and see how you work. You can also invite several of the most impressive business people to school on a panel where they can relate their experiences and ideas for the entire business school. This incidentally, would give you an edge on future employment.

Let's look at other ways to combine interests. A student with a focus both in history and business might do a comprehensive history of a well-established company. If the thesis is good enough, the student might be able to interest the company in publishing it for its own internal use. The student can do more on his or her own—perhaps try to sell it to a local newspaper for adaptation or serialization. This one project might even be a launching pad to a new career—writing histories for other companies much like those writers who produce annual reports.

One caution about writing papers. I can't offer any tips on how to write really well. I can only say emphatically that it's a difficult process. Dorothy Parker said that the only fun in writing comes from having written. In any case, most of us in college write our papers in one draft. We turn it in, receive a grade, and that's it. All writers agree that writing is really rewriting, but few students have the chance to learn that. Therefore, I urge you to learn to discuss your paper with your professor. Go over it together in detail. If it needs work, rewrite it, even though it is not assigned. In the process, you will not only become closer to your professor, you will learn how to develop, shape, and hone ideas.

Think of what Francis Bacon advised in his famous essay on thinking: "More than thinking or speaking, only writing makes you exact." There is another benefit that is less obvious but just as important—something that will stand you in good stead throughout your working life: You will learn to push yourself, putting aside ego in order to work at something. One reason many companies don't want to hire new graduates is that they come to work with the same attitude that they had in school, a "once is enough" syndrome. In business and in professional life, doing and *redoing* are what it takes to get the job done.

Electives

Just as there are behavioral skills to develop, so there are interests to pursue. In this regard, electives can be used to great benefit. Consider an English major whose hobby is cooking. Why not look into home economics courses to augment the possibilities of being a food or cookbook editor or writer, or a food stylist for commercials. The predental student can also be interested in sculpture—a perfect match of the aesthetic and manual skills involved that can lead to complementary careers. The science major may want to understand organizational theory as well as the theories of physics and therefore can take business courses as electives. The urban planning major knows that so much is based on argument and persuasion of political groups and therefore can take every speech and debate course offered.

Identify your interests, anything from inklings to passions, and allow yourself the pleasure and luxury of pursuing what appeals to you. Consider electives, not as easy ways out, but as ideal ways to embroider your course of study with interests that make you more well rounded and happy.

Positive Test-Taking

Now that single task that produces the most high anxiety—exams. Tests appear as regularly as clockwork; yet somehow taking them doesn't get any easier. Fear of being tested is a subject that could be explored in an entire book. Ideally, tests are your forum for presenting what you have learned. And from that point of view alone they are valuable. But there is another aspect of taking exams—more subtle but equally as important as part of your "double agenda"—that is seldom even mentioned: how to present yourself on paper and in person. Obviously I am not talking about objective tests—true/false, multiple choice, etc. There is only one piece of advice I can offer for them—find out who has previously taken either the test given by a specific instructor or a required exam (as GRE, LSAT, SAT) and ask for samples and for patterns for answering. Finding the patterns present in an array of multiple answers is critical; some brilliant test-takers say that they can figure out the right answer from recognizing that it is the only one different from the three or four that are similar.

Subjective tests, or essays, are quite a different matter. It is here that you have a chance to demonstrate who you are to your professor. The trick is not to answer like a robot, spewing out meaningless lists of data, but to offer instead a conceptual framework that shows that you are thoughtful, curious, and knowledgeable.

In a paper entitled, "Examinationship and the Liberal Arts: An Epistemological Inquiry," Professor William Perry of Harvard's Bureau of Study Counsel identifies the polar differences in the way students present themselves through written ideas. Perry's article was written ostensibly to explain a scandalous incident at Harvard. A student took the final exam of a course in which he was never enrolled and by bulling his way through an essay got the only high grade in the class. From this Perry spins his brilliant epistemological theory of how we know what we know. He differentiates between two ways of presenting material—"cowing" and "bulling"—two patterns that students fall into. He defines cowing as endlessly listing data without awareness of its significance and without comment on any context or frames of reference which determine the nature and meaning of the data. Detail and fact are substituted for understanding and interpretation. He defines bulling as a discourse on the context, frames of reference, and points of observation, all of which sounds good but is not supported by data.

Who gets ahead, the "cowers" or "bullers"? Perry believes that the system at least passes the cowers. Instructors have compassion for hours spent in memorization of the data and tend to give cowers the grade of C. However, they will reward bulling with an A if they don't suspect that the wool is being pulled over their eyes; if they do suspect it, then an F. Of course, the proper response is a combination of both. Through interpretation of data we demonstrate our understanding of what we have learned. After all, outside a frame of reference, facts have little meaning.

No one can think that it's fair for the Harvard student to have gotten by with fancy footwork alone, but is it more fair to pass those who have no grasp of the significance of what they are studying? Does memorization equal demonstrated learning? No. We need to have the data or facts at hand, to be sure, and we need to have a point of view, a framework.

Presenting facts within a significant framework requires skill. I asked a variety of students who regularly got A's on their papers to reveal how they presented their answers. Several said that they led off their answer with a classical quote or literary reference that contained the essence of their response. By doing so they demonstrated their ability to synthesize the material and also provided a graceful opening. It was clear that they had taken the time before the test to do some research and include the views of current theorists to show a grasp of contemporary thinking. If they had strong preferences for one school of thought over another, they explained their reasons. In short, they demonstrated to their professors that they had (not only) a complete and thorough knowledge of their material, but also that they fully grasped its meaning and significance.

Oral Examinations

For most people, public speaking brings up the most terrible fears. It is as if revealing what we think aloud and being visible exposes us to mortal danger. Whatever the feeling, real or imagined, there are some ways to take action so that we can appear to be as smart and prepared as we are. Courses in public speaking and debate have helped to prepare many students not only for later careering but also for developing skills in thinking clearly and in leadership. If they are available as electives, take them, even though they sound formidable. They provide valuable training.

There are several tactics that you can teach yourself, however. First, rehearse by listing possible questions that your professor(s) would come up with.

Then prepare comprehensive answers. You must not answer in monosyllabic yes's or no's anymore than you can answer "I don't know." The test is less about getting the critical fact out than it is about determining whether you can handle an answer, in short, whether you are knowledgeable. If, however, you don't know an answer, begin your response by admitting that, then immediately elaborate how you would go about finding out, and where it fits into what you do know.

You can practice your oral answers, just as you would written answers. You certainly can and should refer to others' work, including that of the professor(s) you are addressing. Be complete—have a beginning, middle, and end.

If you are a graduate student preparing for your orals, then you must also prepare to take responsibility for the exam session. What you are being judged for is not only whether you can provide every detail but also whether you present your facts in a significant framework. Let me repeat an incident that I included in *Skills For Success* that is quite appropriate here.

A director of training of a major psychoanalytic institute told me about two young men who had just taken their oral examinations in order to be admitted to the institute. That means that about ten to twelve years after college, medical school, internship, residency, their own psychoanalysis, and several years of special training in the institute, they would again be tested to finally belong. You might assume that they would both pass, but only one did. How was it possible to fail after so much extraordinary time and effort? Here is the question asked of the two men, and the passing and failing responses, so you can understand more about the nature of self-presentation.

The question was asked of both men, independently: "What would you expect a one-year-old baby to do if its mother, upon bringing it to your office, had to leave the room for a few minutes?" The following is the failing response: "I'd expect the baby to cry after being separated from the mother." The passing answer: "I'd expect the baby to cry after being separated from the mother. Separation anxiety is maybe the most complex issue of all our lives, especially obvious in infancy. There are, however, conflicting interpretations. According to these..."

Now, let's look at what happened. At first glance, it appears that the psychiatrists' answers are identical. The facts are there—both agree that the baby cries. But any serious interview or exam doesn't only measure one's ability to state a fact. Often the facts themselves are less important than the interpretation of them, especially in psychiatry. The failing psychiatrist gave an answer and waited obediently; the passing one posited the same answer but then revealed what it meant, in a series of interpretations. He provided a way to let the examiner know that he was prepared, having read extensively. He spoke as a colleague and as a likely credit to the institute. He intuitively knew that the test was a vehicle for such self-presentation.

What the examiner wanted to ask but legally could not was, "Are you enough like us to warrant our letting you join our institute?" The first psychiatrist was not; he showed himself still to be a student. But the second was; he knew, in addition to the facts, how to substantiate his answer with examples from psychiatric theory and practice.

All subjective tests, whether written or oral, are vehicles for self-presentation. The questions are there to provoke a dialogue, a vehicle giving you an opportunity to reveal who you are and what you know.

There are behaviors we must learn. We want not only to be a successful student, but a successful protégé, and thereafter a successful professional. We cannot wait to learn the appropriate behavior until the last minute, for correct behavior encompasses skills that must be developed, just as in sports. If you want to be an expert skier, you would not put on a pair of skis for the first time in front of a judge. That is, of course, preposterous, yet that is exactly what we demand of ourselves in pressured tests, written or oral. We need practice and coaching. And it is up to us to make it happen.

4

Clubs and Activities: The Invisible Curriculum

"Action may not always bring happiness; but there is no happiness without action."
—Disraeli

Clubs and activities have long been called extracurricular activities. "Extra" suggests that they are apart from the real curriculum, and therefore somewhat superfluous. Yet clubs and activities offer a kind of "invisible curriculum" wherein we learn to develop skills that cannot be learned in the classroom. They teach us how to work with people, something that cannot be learned while listening to a lecture, and yet, in life it is just as important as the ability to do the job.

Each event has its significant aspects — planning, design, budgeting, advertising, publicity, and management. There are lessons to be learned which can only come by doing. And in college there is a built-in bonus: You can experiment in a "safe" environment. It is not "sink or swim" as it will be later when you have to support yourself or a family. It is unlikely that you will be fired from a club. So you can feel free to try much more than you would dare on a first job. You can learn: (1) how to persuade a group to a different way of thinking; (2) the high risk of being right at the expense of others' being wrong; (3) the art of compromise and negotiation; and, (4) how to encourage esprit de corps.

In my interviews, successful people from every walk of life—business, arts, science—revealed to me that their ability to make the right decisions at critical turning points in their lives was based on earlier preparatory steps they had taken. All successful people have built their expertise and are always getting ready for the next step, unconsciously or by strategy, even if they don't know what that next step will be.

As graduate or undergraduate students, Achievers were always involved in extracurricular activities. Some were active in debate or theater arts. Some managed radio stations. Others were officers in student government or fraternities. Still others played in the orchestra. What is in a list of activities? Remember back in high school when you joined clubs only to add something to your yearbook biographical sketch? It is not enough to join; you must actively participate. Obviously, Achievers did more than just join. They made something happen. And making things happen—creating opportunities—is a great skill in itself.

It is precisely about learning to make opportunities that I will suggest an action plan in this chapter so that you can get the most out of the Invisible Curriculum. A cautionary word: It is worth the extraordinary effort even if you have to defend your involvement to your friends or family for taking time away from your studies. But remember, these are extracurricular activities and clubs that were the touchstones upon which Achievers based their continuing experiences. Successful people credit extracurricular activities specifically for developing three different skills:

- Building personal courage
- Developing organization savvy or a sense of how to play "office politics"
- Establishing a sense of real professionalism

These key factors are not yet taught in college, not even in M.B.A. programs or law school—though they certainly belong there. Academic learning needs to be integrated with an awareness of how things work in the world. The "how" is a complement to the "what" and deserves recognition, attention, and inclusion.

Personal Style

By the time we are in college, most of us already have developed a sense of fashion. Each of us knows what to wear when; we are able to choose hot weather clothes, interview suits, formal attire, beach wear. Opportunities in later life coupled with fashion guides will keep changing our sense of style. Fashion is one way of visibly presenting ourselves. But ultimately, "apparel oft proclaims the man" was wrong advice, as specious as the rest that double-dealing Polonius gave to Hamlet. Putting on a three-piece suit may get you in the interview door, but it does not guarantee that you'll get into graduate school or get hired for the job you want. What really counts is your self-presentation, your behavior. But we have little training in developing a "wardrobe of behaviors."

Clubs and Activities: The Invisible Curriculum

Most of us develop one way of interacting, and as a result, get stuck acting that one way for a lifetime. If we're sweet and unthreatening, we are always sweet and unthreatening. If we are angry or difficult or arrogant or abrasive, we play out that personality like a robot or broken record.

We need to develop a wardrobe of behaviors, just like our wardrobe of clothes. One of the best ways, if not *the* best way, for students is to begin to practice these steps through extracurricular activities. These activities are safe places to test ourselves so we will know about when to be forceful and when not to be, when to take the lead and when to be supportive, how to handle conflict within a group. These skills, which are the basis of "style," are critical. In fact, they are life skills. We need to start developing them early.

How does one develop a particular style? Is it calculated or does it just happen? Psychologists theorize about personality — is it inherited or learned from people around us, our family and friends? Do we pick it up from magazines and other media? Or is it a combination of all these factors? Why is it that we are willing to change our hairstyles but not our behavior? Most of us act as if personality were given, fixed, and not to be experimented with.

But observe how different we are when we are selling a car than when we are buying one, talking to our professors or to our parents, or to those students who are more knowledgeable than others. Does this mean that we are chameleons without character? On the contrary, it indicates that we adapt and naturally develop appropriate roles that enable us to choose who to be and how to act depending on the situation. You might argue that this sounds manipulative. But isn't it wiser to take charge of a situation than to be locked into only one way of acting or, worse, reacting. Playing a broken record removes the joy of spontaneous reaction, not only for you, but also for the people around you. And that leaves you totally predictable, ultimately powerless and boring.

Let's look at the change in a top engineering student who had wanted to be an engineer ever since childhood. Jim's father had shared and encouraged his son's dream of a career in engineering as a means of escape from a limited rural background. Had he kept his early dream intact, with blinders on to any other possibility, he would be an engineer today. That is, of course, not a bad choice in itself. But good choices have more to do with personal interest and abilities. Active in student politics, Jim became a campus leader during the fifties when college life was rolling along smoothly. His position, however, required him to resolve and mediate conflicts between officers, deal with unpopular issues, apprise his sponsors and professors of the student body government decisions, invite provocative guests to campus meetings. From the simple act of becoming student body officer, Jim discovered new potential in himself. He became a confident leader with a pronounced talent for management. He tried out a new role and succeeded in it. There was some cost nonetheless; there are always trade-offs in life. Jim sacrificed straight-A grades and nearly lost his chance for the one engineering position he really wanted. Eventually, the company hired him anyway. They were more impressed with his political experience and placed him in a management program. Today he heads a major program at one of the nation's leading institutions. Looking back, he recognizes that having been student body president changed his entire life.

Most of the successful lawyers I interviewed attributed their skills at persuading juries and judges, as well as presenting themselves forcefully to clients and other lawyers, to their early active participation in drama club. Acting, they claimed, helped them to break out of their shells. And it is not surprising that lawyers are interested in acting; after all, you could say the courtroom itself creates drama. But think of the possibilities for business, science, and art majors. Besides teaching some of the great lines of literature, which are often not taught in regular courses, drama clubs offer a good first step in career advancement—learning to overcome the fear of being in front of an audience.

John joined the Future Teachers of America Club even though he was not overly excited about the prospects of becoming a member of what he regarded as a declining profession. He joined with half a heart and, I might add, with only half a mind; he was really absent during the meetings he attended. He went through the motions of being a member. He paid his dues and attended the meetings, but sat in them like the proverbial bump on a log, volunteering nothing, chairing nothing, asking nothing, and contributing nothing. Upon graduation, he was unable to find a teaching job that suited him.

It wasn't that the field of education was a bad choice. The president of the Future Teachers of America didn't have the same result. Because she had already established a reputation prior to graduation, she was sought after by both the public school and a community college system. Over her last several years at school, she invited important guest speakers with whom she stayed in contact; she researched alternative curricula for colleges; she familiarized herself with the different jobs of president, counselor, and instructor at a small college; she created opportunities for club members through internships; and she sponsored a series of dinner meetings with faculty so that active students could get a glimpse of the inside world of higher education. She also asked the influential people she had come to know to write letters of recommendation for her, which they were happy to do. So it was much more than luck that landed her her first full-time college position—though it seemed that way to people who didn't know her.

Contrast these two antithetical experiences. John came to the club expecting to be "done to"—informed, educated, and placed—while the other came expecting to create something and help build a successful group. This club, like most organizations, offered each member the same opportunities. One took advantage and benefited—the other did not.

If you want something to happen, you have to make it happen. This may sound clichéd, but it is so. Life is indeed what you make it. Certainly we can all see this with our perfect twenty-twenty hindsight. Kierkegaard wrote that we understand life only in reverse but are forced to live it forward. But we can, and often do, benefit from others' experiences. Furthermore, we can each set up experiments for ourselves. We can begin with clubs and activities, internships, part-time jobs, individual courses, and seminars, seizing every chance to shape and reshape ourselves according to what we want most. It all has to do with our intent to try, and even to risk being foolish to create our own possibilities.

Times are hard. There is no doubt about that—even Ph.D.'s often cannot find the teaching or research positions that their training prepares them for. Many have had to pursue other careers when they have been unemployed for months. To change that situation, a group of unemployed Ph.D.'s, graduates of a major institution, formed an association, the purpose of which was to make their plight public. They were sympathetically interviewed in the local newspapers and talk shows. They held monthly meetings and invited guest speakers to help them.

I was one such speaker. As I began to present alternatives to teaching, I noticed that they were recording my presentation for their newsletter. They were behaving like any association—trying to improve themselves, expand in size and scope, including producing a comprehensive monthly newsletter. But this was a group that should have expected to dissolve once the members could find jobs! Perhaps a more productive course would have been getting into the career development business. They could have invited each member who did find work to come back with a map of what he or she actually did, or sought help in starting up a short internship program to fuse academic theory with business practice—chemistry with oil companies; applied art with advertising; history with corporate libraries or newspapers.

Why didn't they do this? As high-minded academicians they held the business community in contempt. But with universities not hiring professors, they needed to reexamine their beliefs in order to achieve their goal of employment. Had they used their university time more creatively and productively, allowing time for varied activities, they might well have had a broader view of alternatives. Had they participated in extracurricular activities, their connections and experiences might have provided the employment opportunities they sought.

How to Find Out Who You Are and What You Want to Be

First, know that you don't have to make only one choice. You can be many things in this life—you may wear several hats at the same time, and then you may change direction altogether. But you must begin. You might start by becoming involved in several different efforts so that you can find out what appeals to you and to what extent you want to be involved. You will find that participating in athletics and music is quite different from the production of a radio show or newspaper or running for a student political office. Athletics or the performing arts can be excellent choices if you have the talent. Given that talent, you have to have what it takes to be part of a group that essentially creates harmony together, whether it is a symphony orchestra, a jazz band, football team, or debating club. All offer the possibility of a great many different kinds of experiences. An All-American basketball star told me that his greatest learning experience came during the period he was benched. Despondent during that difficult year, he learned to cheer on his team members. Only then could he understand that a large part of his value and purpose came in supporting his team members and not just playing well himself.

On any athletic team there are players who are known as the best performers, the most valuable, the most supportive or popular—and each of them complements the team. Understanding who we are and how we fit in is vital to our own development. For example, if you are a member of the band but not the leader, you still have many chances to contribute. You may be the one who finds unusual music, the one who gets the campus newspaper to review the group, or the one who contacts professional musicians off campus to listen to and advise the group. Or you might be the one who cooks chili and generates enthusiasm, support—esprit de corps.

Being involved in the production of a campus newspaper or radio show offers a variety of jobs. If you are creative, you can be writer, performer, or both. If you are interested in public relations and advertising, you can assume the responsibility of selling the production to the potential audience and, in doing so, learn about the world of public relations or advertising. If you are interested in management, there is that chance plus the potential to make connections with professors, administrators, and the entire outside community. These activities can become virtual minibusinesses as can fund-raising events, homecomings, and alumni weeks.

Clubs and Activities: The Invisible Curriculum

A small group of students interested in studying business might start an investment club or a small enterprise, creating the perfect chance to seek out professors as advisors. In this way they can learn both how to relate and how to perform. At this very moment, all over America, students are playing the stock market, catering parties, publishing neighborhood guides, moving other students out of and into apartments. Remember, college is a laboratory, and within it are an extraordinary variety of opportunities for experiments of all kinds. And many professors are willing to act as coaches.

All of these activities also offer chances to find out what you like and what you don't like, what you need to learn and what you already know. If you discover you care more about the creation and sales of the concept by yourself than you do working together with a team, you might lean toward entrepreneurialism rather than large corporate business. Only by experimenting can you find clues toward answering that most perplexing of questions: "What am I going to do when I finish college?"

Using Professional Associations

Many professional associations sponsor and support professional clubs for students majoring in the field —engineers, nurses, dentists, teachers, and more. Getting to know professionals in the field is an invaluable source of contacts. The possibility of participation in regional and national conventions affords you a chance to see who's who in the profession as well as to keep abreast of the latest technical developments in the field.

For example, a group of engineering students held a preprofessional seminar just before the national convention of engineers. I was invited to attend the seminar and conduct a workshop for the students. One of the engineering students was particularly interesting to me because of her questions and ideas.

Later, during the national convention, I invited her to appropriate meetings and meals. As a result, her own charisma became evident to some of the practicing engineers. One took an interest in her and helped her obtain employment in a chemical division of a large manufacturing company.

As a side benefit, she has kept me apprised of her movement and success. I have enjoyed every letter and call. Professionals and student sponsors all share the same sense of joy from watching a student take risks and grow. And these actions embolden all of us to take more chances in our own lives and to encourage our friends, colleagues, and families to do the same.

Leadership

The political arena of student government represents another major area for volunteer activity. Successful people who have entered a race for student
office, regardless of whether or not they win, agree
that the experience was more worthwhile than they
could have dreamed. First, they learned to risk their
own egos. It takes courage to lay your ideas on the
line and set yourself up for criticism and possible
defeat, which is what you do when you run for office.
Secondly, they learned how to create a team of the
people who agreed to support them. It takes courage
to ask people not only for their vote, but also to
campaign for you. Third, it teaches you to be there
when the votes are counted. If you don't win, you

must be a gracious loser and congratulate your opponent and offer him or her your support; if you do win, then you must begin to act on your campaign promises. Winning is an honor, but it is not an end in itself—it is another beginning, a real chance to push forward and make things happen.

"Coming through" is a skill in itself to be practiced, tested, and realized. And that is not all. Leadership demands public speaking, which in turn means you must be able to think on your feet. It demands expertise in motivating others, redirecting functions or events, and experimenting with appropriate compromises with opposing factions. Only with hands-on experience can you understand how the process of leadership actually works.

In assuming leadership roles in most student organizations, you have the privilege of working under the direction of a sponsor who is, one hopes, savvy, wise, and connected. You can expect to have additional entree to professors, administration, alumni, other club presidents, and the outside world in a much broader scope and with greater ease than others might have.

Involvement in student government can, for example, lead to the larger political world, starting with volunteer work on a politician's campaign, clerkships, internships, even graduate school. It is no accident that many top executives, professionals, and community leaders were political leaders as college and graduate students. Ability to lead is the hallmark of the Achiever. The skill that it takes can be developed, nurtured, and made a part of a person's repertoire. Leadership and leadership roles are integrated into the social fabric of our society.

* * *

We've been talking about getting top roles to practice leadership. But running for office or chairing a committee is not the only way. Learning how to support that designated leader is a critical skill and naturally precedes the actual taking of power.

If your own goal is to be leader, you'll learn how to play out that role more effectively by assisting leader first. Or, if your goal is to be a good team player—there are infinitely more chances for this—then you can take these same practice sessions. Remember that a supportive role is not a passive one. You don't give up the human trait of "acting" for one of only re-acting. Rather, you learn that nobody makes it alone without support—from game planning to morale building. Being supportive requires tremendous attention to the goals and behavior of the leader, to be sure, but also to the group and the outside arena—the rest of the college.

A Special Note to Women

Women are still viewed in supporting, not leadership, roles. While these beliefs are changing, old habits die hard. Change is resisted hard even in those of us who want it most. During my years as a management consultant to large corporations, part of my work has been to train employees to be more active. I design problem-solving exercises to develop initiative and leadership skills. I give a task of working out the best solution to small, leaderless groups of people. At the completion of the task, the real work begins. I always ask the person who emerged as the leader to rise. Invariably, this is what happens: When the group is all male, one man will stand immediately. When I ask why he feels that he was the leader, he answers the way every leader does: He initiated the discussion, took notes, shaped the format, focused the discussion when there were too many tangents, facilitated group participation, summarized the decisions, and accomplished the task within the given time. When a male is a leader in a mixed group, the same thing happens.

But when the leader of a mixed group is a woman, she is usually reluctant to stand up in the first place and needs the active encouragement of her group to claim her leadership role. When she does concede that she was the leader, she reports the same activities as her male counterparts. The only difference is her reluctance to claim that she was the leader.

In an all-female group, someone usually says that there was no leader and that the entire group participated equally. But when I ask who has taken the responsibility for facilitating, guiding, redirecting, in short, focusing the group, one woman—usually the one who originally declared that there was no leader—will stand.

What is this really about? You can see that there are few differences in the way men and women describe their leadership qualities. So it is not that women are less qualified to be leaders than men, because as leaders, they perform the same leaderlike acts. The major difference lies in women's having a harder time, socially and psychologically, accepting themselves in the role of leader. Women students must work doubly hard to overcome this reluctance and seek out specific opportunities to practice leadership.

5

Using the Outside: Working and Internships

"Work is less boring than amusing oneself."
—Claude Baudelaire

Working is a vital part of the invisible curriculum, but it can be a double-edged sword. Whether on campus or off, full- or part-time, paid internship, or not, work offers extraordinary possibilities for learning, experimentation, connection, and even profit. But there are drawbacks. Work is time-consuming and potentially energy-draining, and can take hours away from study and social time. But that is the worst of it. The best has no limits:

• Work provides active hands-on experience, often a welcome change from passive lecture attendance and note taking.
• It allows a battered ego to experience relief as roles are switched from anxious test-taker to doer.

(This is particularly true for older returning students who are used to autonomy and responsibility.)

• Work exposes you to something new.

• A job can affirm your career decision and speed you on.

• Or it can prove you wrong in your choice and therefore become a catalyst in redirection.

• It allows relationships with peers and supervisors to develop, providing a sample of teamwork.

• Work furnishes a laboratory in which to test theories learned in class and presents situations in which to practice solving real problems.

• It offers a student the opportunity to bring experiences to bear on classroom work, thereby enriching it.

• Ultimately, it serves as a bridge, building the transition between college and career.

Not working is not an inspiring alternative.

Let's consider the notion of using work for more than one purpose. Students who work at part-time or summer jobs just to pay expenses live in a double world: work vs. college. This is a tough dichotomy that too many apply later: work vs. life. Instead, seek out jobs that interest and expand you. For example, a district attorney who had never lost a case told me part of the secret of his success. To supplement a partial college scholarship, he worked as a clerk in a department store. Bored, he decided to experiment to see if he could differentiate those customers who would buy something from those who were just browsing. When he perfected this skill, he stepped up his experiment. He then tried to sell the non-buyers. In the process, he taught himself the psychology of sales, motivation, and persuasion—skills that he could easily use as a lawyer, successfully persuading judges and juries.

Think of it. Whether you work in a department store, a fast-food chain, a gas station, a government office—you have before you a rich experimental field. In addition, it is ripe for anything you want to study or have been assigned. Our district attorney could have written up his findings for papers in psychology or marketing or business courses. He could have published his field research in the campus newspaper, a marketing journal, or even the local newspaper business section. Still, what he did enriched and emboldened him plus paid for living expenses.

Internships

On almost all campuses the career placement center, which traditionally provided placement after graduation, has grown in scope. Now career planning programs have been developed which also offer and administer internships.

Were I to prescribe what should be included in every college or graduate school curriculum, no matter the area of study, I would insist on internships as a true, practical complement to classroom theory.

Internships typically are short-term, fairly menial jobs within an organization, paid or not, that serve to acquaint you with what that organization does and simultaneously give it a chance to see whether you fit in. You can be assigned as a "gofer," a kind of errand runner to perform small tasks for anyone who needs something done, or you can be assigned to work on one special project. Both have their advantages. Being assigned at large lets you see, albeit superficially, more of what goes on within the organization and opens the door for you to make connections with any number of people. On the other hand, getting a specific assignment gives you direct experience in learning the difficulties and rewards of working together with a team. You become better known to the people you work with because the group is smaller.

The oldest and most traditional internship program is in medicine, where internship (and residencies) are prerequisites to becoming licensed in the field. While medical internships usually follow an intense graduate program, law students usually intern during their summers, most often between the second and third years. Law students fortunate enough to acquire internships may be offered positions with their respective law firms following graduation. Everyone thinks that that is success in itself, but I wonder. Isn't the acceptance of interns to join a firm after graduation something like a prearranged marriage? Wouldn't it be better to view it as a trial or test association? This suggests a certain easy acceptance on the part of the interns; you know, "a bird in the hand...." I would advise students to seek multiple interviews with potential employers in order to make the best possible choice. "Going steady" is as much a tryout of the process as it is of the mate.

In a manner similar to the law internship, many business organizations now employ students. If this does not happen in your field, bring it to the attention of your professors, who might persuade local companies or professional organizations to introduce this policy. It is well worth the effort.

Why would any organization want a student around? First of all, what better way to identify potential talent and to establish a reservoir of qualified future employees. Secondly, students bring the latest in academic theory and technology to the company, and that is no insignificant contribution.

Internships are often established by a university in cooperation with local businesses. In Los Angeles, for example, both the radio and television industries extend a diversity of internships to college and university departments in the areas of communication, cinema, and journalism. The architecture internships at the University of Southern California are highly coveted. A few institutions, such as Antioch and the University of Cincinnati, have pioneered work/study programs in which a paid job in the student's area of study is substituted for regular course work for a semester, or sometimes a full year. Course credit is given for this work. Smith College has instituted over two hundred internships for their liberal arts undergraduate women.

In California, some colleges and universities participate in a program called the Educational Participation in Communities, whose stated purpose is to offer students real-life work experience as a means of developing job skills and exploring career options while taking part in community problem-solving.

If your school has no established internship program, you can initiate one yourself. Find an organization for which you would like to work, and offer yourself as an intern. If you need help, then solicit the assistance of your best-known professors, who may themselves be consultants to companies within the areas of your interests. These same professors are likely to have direct contact and large networks of associates and colleagues. They can get you started.

Using Internships as Direction-Finders

If you really don't have a clear notion of what you want to do following graduation, an internship can help clarify your uncertainties and focus your interests. How do you know which organizations to consider? The answer, of course, is all kinds— newspapers, hospitals, radio and television stations, emergency help centers, political organizations, religious groups, retail stores, import-export businesses, libraries, schools, advertising and public relations agencies, factories, labor unions, financial firms—in short, all kinds of small and large businesses, arts, services, professions. Choose the one closest to your own interests and course of study. You are actually engaged in a quest to find your direction. You want to test yourself, to find your talents and aptitudes. Or, if you have not been able to identify a goal and feel unable to define what it is you want to do, then find some kind of job—start anywhere—and look for aspects of the work that absorb you more than others. Life offers all of us more surprises in the discovery of our interests than we expect.

Lee, an environmental geography major, worked part-time in her university's law library to pay for her tuition. She, however, was quite passionless about her courses and her work; a terrible situation that too many of us endure for too long. Early in her junior year, she decided to risk an internship in an area she enjoyed reading about. She volunteered to work for the city planning council and discovered to her joy that she had "come home;" she experienced a sense of belonging in a field for the first time, a congruence of dream and reality. She then redirected her major and threw herself into her studies while taking on more work at the council. She not only created her own internship, but much more: She was reshaping herself.

You have to realize that Lee didn't just walk in and get assigned to the most interesting project with the most visibility. Not by a long shot. She performed many menial tasks: answering phones, stuffing envelopes, clipping newspaper stories, proofreading papers, and serving generally as a "gofer." She had to forgo her ego, be consistently cheerful, and willing, even eager, to perform without complaint these inherently boring tasks. But consider the whole process. Here she was, part of things, working alongside some of the people she most admired. Lee took the time to ask them about their personal goals and career stories, how they began, why they continued, what else they wanted to do, how they handled office politics, how they made their luck, and what the consequences of their choices were. In addition to her involvement in her work, she had a chance to advance in her course of study and gain perspective on how an office actually works. She also had the unique advantage of seeing role models and possibilities right under her nose. What could be more rewarding, and worth taking a chance for?

As adolescents and college students how do we make our first career choices? Too often we are programed to pursue what is currently in vogue. In the fifties, boys were sent to college to become engineers, and girls studied to be teachers. In the sixties—if they hadn't "dropped out"—boys studied community service, while girls pursued social work. In the seventies, boys went to computer science or law school, and girls began to study law or entered M.B.A. programs in significant numbers. But the result of not making choices based on personal commitment is that too many people come out of school unstimulated, dissatisfied, and still undecided about what to do with their degrees. Myths about how people actually perform in different jobs abound. Television and films have stereotyped medicine and police work. Students are expected to choose a career without having any experience to draw upon. We are, therefore, consumed with illusions about work. Like that old line about understanding modern art, we expect of career choices that we will "know it when we see it."

Some words of comfort: People who don't know what it is they want to do are not stupid. Some years ago the Higher Education Research Institute at

UCLA run by Alexander and Helen Astin found differences between those female students who came to college with preset career goals and majors, and those who were undecided. The undecided students turned out to be more intelligent and flexible, finally making appropriate choices after experiencing trial and error.

Look at what happens to people who really have used internships in an experimental way. From the first time he listened to music on the radio, Gary had wanted to be a disc jockey. It seemed to him that deejays were powerful and had simply the best jobs in the world. His dreams came true in college when he landed an internship with a local radio show station that played Top 40 hits. As an intern he was required to do a variety of tasks that were quite different from the job of deejay: delivering the mail, running errands, helping on a promotion campaign, and finally substituting for a vacationing salesperson. He discovered, to his amazement, that these other jobs were significant, and, more importantly, that marketing and sales were his real talents. Redirecting his childhood dream, he became a successful marketing person. The internship was his "direction-finder." Taking the risk of interning at a radio station revealed to him jobs that he would not have thought of before.

Here's another kind of internship experience—one that revealed that a particular field was totally wrong. Richard had always wanted to be a teacher. He gladly signed up for a student teaching position, the traditional internship in the education field. While he was teaching history in a public high school in a mid-sized city, Richard realized that he had made a bad choice for himself. He didn't have enough patience for his students, he disliked the slow pace of teaching, and he felt constrained by the restrictions in text selection. At the end of student teaching, he promptly shifted gears. Richard volunteered his services to the local newspaper and became an intern doing special reporting on education. Because of his teaching experience, his proposal for a special series was accepted. During his time at the paper, he sought out news reporters for advice. He was hired by one of those reporters, who had been promoted to editor. Two attempts gave Richard the chance to know more about his own interests and style and served him in the very best way.

Another story about second thoughts belongs to Donna. She had chosen psychology as an undergraduate major but was heartsick that her classroom theory did not match her fantasy of the drama of psychotherapy. As a last chance to test herself before she changed majors, Donna interned at a local crisis clinic. There she was supervised while taking incoming calls on the hotline. After she proved herself able, she was invited to assist a group counselor, then trained to be a lay therapist. By the time she graduated, she had a caseload of her own clients. This experiment affirmed her original choice and saved her career. This intervention also taught her about the nature of experimenting itself. She is a much better supervisor now than she would ever have been.

Externships

Some colleges are experimenting with a relatively new development in career planning designed to help people sort out career goals called "externships." Students are matched with alumni or alumnae for meetings that can take place over a lunch hour, a day, or even a week, during which the alumni agree to share their career experiences and professional insights. That way a student gets a close-up, insider's view of a profession, warts and all, and can perhaps reject certain choices and decide to pursue others without the direct experience.

I managed a brilliantly conceived conference whose purpose was just that. Designed by D. Sam Scheele and called Alternative Pursuits to America's Third Century, the conferencing process provided participants technical assistance to plan and implement their own community service or other projects. But first they had to "be someone else for a day." This exercise required conferees from all over the country and walks of life to pick several careers that most interested them. Then they had to find and mingle with people in that field, following them around, and generally closely observing what they actually did during the course of a day. The response was tremendous. People found that their illusions were shattered. One psychologist, for example, had thought that investigative reporting was the most stimulating job imaginable, one against which he had always measured his own career. To his amazement, he found that tracking down clues was quite a boring and ultimately unrewarding process. He reassessed what he was doing and revised his advice to patients about defining one's vocation from fantasy without first checking it out.

Another participant, a social worker, took the opposite route and chose what she thought was the worst occupation, waitressing. Going to a local diner to observe the waitress, she discovered that her subject did much more than just take orders and bring on the eggs. The waitress was literally an on-the-spot social worker, joking with regular customers in an easy style, asking about their lives, sympathizing with their problems, cheering their progress. It was a revelation to this professional woman, whose job meant helping people, and gave her a completely new perspective on her work. She had learned the lesson of humility.

As you can see, both internships and externships offer a rich opportunity. If you accept an internship, don't complain that your assigned task is too lowly, that you aren't appreciated, that the work is too complicated for such a minimal (or no) wage, or that the assignment is too short. Take it as it comes. Be eager and ready to help. Make friends, but don't take sides in office politics. Save questions for casual, off-work times, like lunch or breaks. And don't ask for career advice too often from your co-workers. And remember to ask about what courses would be good background for the field, which to omit, how to gain entry to your chosen career, what to consider in choosing a career. Ask them for stories about their professional experience and the nature of the work. Be interested, but don't be a pest. You'll not only be learning how to get along with people in an office situation, but you'll also be increasing your awareness of your field and turning the job into the beneficial and rewarding experience it should be.

6

Commencing: The End of the Beginning

"You won't skid if you stay in a rut."
—Kin Hubbard

At the beginning of this book I referred to college as an experiment in hope and risk. It can be a unique opportunity for students who are alert and interested enough to take the chance to shape their fantasies as well as shape themselves in the image of their fantasies. These ideas of who and what we want to be can be very strong within us, or they can be a long time in the making, needing development and nurturing to make themselves known. Identifying our dreams is a continuing process in life because we grow and change. But the skills we need to cultivate a fantasy and shape it into reality continue to be the same. All the proposed activities in the preceding chapters about mentor relationships, clubs, student government, internships, part-time work, strategic papers and projects, are meant to help you learn to expose yourself to the world in order that you might learn about yourself and your dreams. The activities and exercises described in the previous chapters should serve to help you discover who you are and discover your interests, skills, even passions. It should be clear to you now that in addition to simply giving you a degree, college is an experience that can help you learn about the world and your place in it.

College commencement is literally our moving-on—on to the world of work, on to a full-time career. *Career* is the word these days, not *job*. It implies a greater constellation, more significant than simply performing one task for pay so that we can live. For many people today, our work is our identity. We experience life through our chosen frameworks. Scientists view the world differently from artists or corporate managers. What we do becomes who we are.

You have been living these past years as a student, thinking of yourself as a "student." Finally the time comes to make an enormous transition and assume a new identity. But change is frightening for everyone. Indeed, adjusting to new circumstances is anxiety-provoking; seeing ourselves in new situations may lead to identity crises that are difficult to live through. There is no shortcut. Everyone who changes goes through it. But these awkward times can be shorter-lived if you begin in college to develop some skills to see you through.

If you are graduating soon, think of this transition period as something akin to growing pains—temporarily painful but endured for a desired result. So how do you go about making the transition from school, no matter how sophisticated the program, to your first postschool job? One way is to use the career planning and development center ever present on college campuses. Here is a description of the services available through them.

Vocational Testing

Every center provides vocational testing for a vast number of students who simply don't know what they want to do. This kind of testing is limited— tests can tell students only what they have been doing and are already fairly adept at; they cannot predict future interests or skills, nor can they know the current marketplace or predict its future. They are limited to jobs and careers known only when the test was created. After all, according to the Department of Labor, one-third of all careers are newly created every decade. That's a lot of new careers to update. But despite their limitations, sometimes vocational tests can be useful. If you don't have any clues, they can at least provide a start. You can use them as you would a fortune-teller. If they tell you what you profoundly want to hear, they're right; if they don't, they're wrong. In that way you can get to see glimmerings of yourself in a process much like panning for gold, to find insight when there isn't clear awareness. Not knowing what you want or not seeing it isn't as rare as you might guess. As a former labor negotiator, I can tell you that the most difficult problem of all is getting people to realize what they really want, not what they think they want or know what others want for them. Try this out. It's harder than you would think.

Career Counselors

Each career center is staffed with a group of people called career counselors. They have often been psychological counselors first, working with students' personal problems. So they care. They have usually had some training in vocational testing. A good counselor makes contacts in the business, arts, and service communities both on and off the campus. They can be great sources of support and powerful allies. Counselors can offer career suggestions, set up meetings with prominent people in any given field, rehearse you before such meetings, assist you in writing your resume, and coach you in ways to present yourself to recruiters and other interviewers. They need to be cultivated, however; so take the initiative and begin discussions.

Counseling Center Services

Use career counselors and centers early. Don't wait until the final month before graduation to make your first appointment. Your freshman year is not too early to start. Counseling centers offer regular seminars in career planning. Make a regular assignment each semester to find out the range of seminars—from choosing a career to preparation for interviews to selection of internships. These seminars can also provide a basis for starting a relationship with the counselor. In addition to "in-house" seminars, you will often find panels where the center invites business and community people in to talk about their own careers and opportunities. Don't miss them nor pass up the opportunity to talk to the panelists. They are a great source of contacts.

Resume-writing workshops, in which you draft a resume, perhaps for the first time in your life, are quite popular. Most employers want a resume that fairly represents your education, work experience, and relevant activities. This one-page précis is harder to write than it seems, so most students welcome assistance by a trained counselor.

Remember that a resume is not what gets you the job; it is only a tool. Writing it does help you be explicit about what you have done, and it legitimizes you better than a business card. But avoid the trap that most people fall into. They finely hone a resume, mail out hundreds, then sit back falsely lulled into believing that they have done their job hunting. Not true. In most cases you won't be called. The fact is that few potential employers respond to any resume. It is passive, noninteractive, and can easily be filed away to be taken care of "later." And if they do respond, you must remember that your resume is competing with hundreds of others.

So, what is a graduating student to do? Certainly do write a resume that is clean and professional, not ostentatious or pompous (no calligraphy or cream-colored parchment of three pages).

Include the following information on a one-page, clearly readable resume:

1. *Name, address, phone.* If you live on campus but will return to another address, label that "permanent" and include it. Do not include age, sex, health, physical size, religion, or marital status.

2. *Education.* In reverse order, starting from the present, include your educational institution, degrees earned, and date graduated. Include any awards or distinctions, fellowships, scholarships, special grants, etc., that you have received. Include such

honors as law review. Do not write grade point average or class standing (unless you're first or top). Generally, do not include anything below college —no high school information except if you were valedictorian, student body president, or Merit Scholarship winner. Include "other training" such as a special summer institute in political science, but not a single day's assertion training workshop.

3. *Work Experience.* List paid jobs in reverse chronological order, stating position, company, responsibilities and dates worked. Remember to divide the tasks of a job. If you had a newspaper route, then list your duties as: door-to-door solicitation, taking and placing orders, billing, delivery, and collections over a large residential area in the city. Don't mention boss's name, or your own assessment of how you did. Include internships, assistantships, and any volunteer experience in the same manner.

4. Do not worry about writing a job objective, although many resume-writing professionals often advise it. There is no one there to match you with a job. This resume is only to represent you, and in most cases does not, and cannot, sell you.

5. *References.* Indicate that you will furnish them on request. If you have a file ready with your placement service, state that and include the address. Be strategic about which people you ask for letters of recommendation to include in that file. Try for a range of references—a professor in your major area, a supervisor, a faculty administrator, a former employer, and prominent family friend.

But then you must follow through! Send your resumes, with a cover letter in order to set up appointments. Then follow up with a phone call. Only interviewing gets you the job.

Career centers often organize internships. Look for such internships, then, that are already arranged and are posted in your department office as well as in the career center. But you need to do more than just apply. You understand that if the career counselor must choose between one student who has become known and trusted and another student who has never before appeared at the center, the one who is known to the counselor has the cutting edge on a good internship. It is only rational that human beings like and promote people they know. Therefore, don't be afraid that you are imposing by getting a counselor to know you. It is the way he or she can really help.

Placement Offices

The career center also functions as a placement office. Such offices do, in fact, act like employment offices, brokering jobs from the outside to graduating students. Lists of jobs are posted and interviews are scheduled. Many centers offer practice in interviewing. Sign up for a mock interview and request a videotape session so that you can see exactly how you appear to interviewers.

Sign up for every interview that you can, no matter whether you are vitally interested in the company or not. Consider it practice for you to understand what an employer wants to accomplish in the interview. Essentially, it is *not* finding the smartest person for the job, but rather it is finding the right person for the right job. Don't play the good student.

Employers don't want students, they want participating employees. To find them, they ask questions that ostensibly ask you to tell them whether you've had any experience, what your past has been, where you see yourself in five years, what strengths and weaknesses you have, even: "If you were a leaf on a tree, where would you place yourself?" These are all strategic questions to get you to answer the implicit (even illegal) question that is really what they want to know: Are you enough like them to make them want to make you a member of their team? They want you to be similar to them in values, intent, background, vision. You must tell, by selecting events from your life, how your experiences in school activities, part-time jobs, relevant interests, and internships demonstrate these attributes and values.

Does this sound too manipulative to you? Then, consider how you pick a friend. You want that person to like you and value your ideas and feelings. The more you share the same ideas and feelings, no matter how different you may appear, the closer you are. There is a saying that we think smart people are those who think we are smart. That's pretty true. If you don't think so, then think of whom you have asked for advice about which professor to study with or which course to take. I'd be willing to bet that you only ask those whose tastes and judgments are the same as yours. You want someone who will validate and support your own instincts about what to do. That is not idiosyncratic behavior. We all do it.

In addition to demonstrating similar values, you have to actively participate in the interview itself. It is not a one-way test, but a dialogue. You too have to come prepared with questions to ask about the company and about the interviewer. Pretend you are interviewing him or her for your newspaper and show at least that much interest. At the end of the interview, obviously thank the interviewer for his or her time. If you want the job, say so. Then ask what their thoughts and feelings are. Ask if there is any concern they have about you so that you have a chance to defend yourself face-to-face and make a stronger pitch. Suppose they think you should have had some more experience, then you can quickly scan your past for activities you participated in, offices you ran for, or projects you undertook in class. Your enthusiasm and demonstration often work. It is always better to present yourself forcefully than to secretly hope they will discover the real, talented, wonderful you. And after all, you are just beginning. If you feel some tension, you might also ask how they got their start, and who gave them a break.

Career counselors can offer strategies and tactics. They may have a library of videotapes of interviews, both good and bad, with which to compare yourself. And they are there to advise you. If you have a bad experience, review it with them so that you can learn for next time.

Successful Careering

Is "career" so different from "success"? One of the meanings of *career* is "progress through life." One of the meanings of *success* is, "one thing after another," like the succession of presidents. Eureka! They are synonymous; both imply growth and movement, not fixed or static attainment. These definitions ought to provide us fresh insight to help us deal with the inevitable choices we face immediately after college or graduate school and then throughout our lives. The Department of Labor predicts that we will all move through three to five different careers. There is much to do for each of us.

Use the services and people in the career development centers. It is a good habit to learn to ask for help when you need it. Remember, no one makes it alone. No one has to make choices alone either. If you look carefully at the biographies of well-known people you will see the connections, negotiations, and risks that link one person to another, catapult one person from one step to another. If you don't risk, you live tied to that false god of self-reliance. While it is true that you alone will do something, you don't pull yourself up by your own bootstraps. The bootstrap myth is unrealistic. My life's work has been devoted to discovering how people do what they do. I have found that each of us is inspired, nourished, encouraged, cheered, confirmed, even transformed, by the deeds, suggestions, and love of others in addition to the will to try for ourselves. Something of everything is open to you if you want it.

20/20 Hindsight: How Sixteen People Used College to Their Advantage

"Experience is not what happens to a
man. It is what a man does with what
happens to him."
—Aldous Huxley

If proof is what you need to get started, then this chapter is for you. Through mapping some successful people's lives, I have found that no matter what period of their lives you look at, they have always experimented and taken risks. Though many people ask me about "late bloomers," I have never seen complete dormancy followed suddenly by full-blown achievement. In reality, we don't fit the cocoon-to-butterfly metaphor. Instead, I have found that Achievers have a will to achieve even when they are in the developmental form of "getting their act together."

I asked people from medicine, science, sports, architecture, publishing, film, radio and television writing, news and production, business, law, and academia to tell me about themselves. I wanted to know what they did in college and graduate school beyond going to class and passing their courses, even if they were brilliant students. So I asked what activities they were involved in; which clubs they belonged to; who were key mentors; what long-term projects, internships, and work experiences were instrumental to their careers. The rest of this chapter contains those answers, which can serve as guideposts to point the way and get you started.

First, I asked everyone how they would approach college if they had a chance to do it all over again. Their answers were surprisingly similar: They all said that they would do nothing differently because each connection they made and activity in which they participated had turned out to be valuable in later life. All agreed that their college experience was a significant part of their formative years. Almost everyone, that is.

One exception worth looking at: Harlan Ellison. A well-known writer, Ellison readily admits to having been thrown out of Ohio State University in 1954 with what he believes is the lowest grade-point average in the history of that institution: .086.

Ellison has written thirty-eight books, has been translated into sixteen languages, has won innumerable awards for his fiction, television scripts, and newspaper columns, is listed in *Who's Who in the World*, regularly lectures at universities like Harvard, Yale, MIT and even Ohio State. Why did this prolific and imaginative author and activist do so badly in college, so that even today, almost thirty years later, he remembers the time as "the most personally debilitating year and a half of my life, a period so dismal and miserable that I felt like some sort of alien thing dropped into a world of darkness.

So much time and emphasis was placed on competing, in areas that held no relation to what I wanted to do with my life, that I found myself expending energy just trying to keep up with scholastic races I didn't want to run. Like many young people, I was socially graceless and was not equipped to combat the peer-group pressures that made anyone not interested in football games, fraternity beer bashes, and seducing coeds feel as if he was a wimp.

"I went to college to get the skills to write. I needed to be exposed to a community of ideas. What I desperately sought in those ivy-covered halls of academe was challenge, intellectual stimulation, exposure to the depth and range of knowledge possessed by all the erudite magicians who had been assembled there to open the world for me. Instead, what I found was teaching by rote, inordinate concern with status, that strange inability of the 1950s to commit to the larger world of which college should have been a hub, and a striking lack of passion. I wanted to be tested, to go through the fire and emerge an adult.

"But the most pernicious aspect of life in the world of college in the 1950's was that nowhere could I find validation for those personal qualities I held dearest: courage, ethics, the power to dream. College life and the unspoken tenets proffered as worthiest of our attention dealt with security (get a high-paying job in some safe industry), true love (get married, have 2.6 babies, a Cadillac convertible, and fit the mold of your parents, even if their lives were demonstrably unsatisfying), and looking good (dress in style, say the same things everyone else was saying, don't stick out of the crowd)."

Ellison's comments pour out in a diatribe against

a conformist system. Students have long been criticized for maintaining the outlook of obedient children, substituting the university for daddy. Growing up, accepting responsibility for one's future, is an awesome and frightening undertaking. But it is a struggle to which students must commit themselves so that they don't dream false dreams of security.

Here, then, are models of courage as demonstrated in the lives of Achievers—proof positive that college offers a laboratory for experimentation, discovery, and connection.

Helen S. Astin

Assistant Provost,
College of Letters and Sciences, UCLA;
author; lecturer; university activist; psychologist.
Adelphi College, B.A., Psychology, 1953
Ohio University, M.S., 1954
University of Maryland, Ph.D., 1957

Q. *As an undergraduate at Adelphi, were you involved in any outside activities?*
A. I was a foreign student, new from Greece. I could hardly speak English, as I remember. I chose to work in the graduate library in psychology, a very positive and strategic choice to get to know the top echelon of students and professors.

Q. *Any mentors in undergraduate study?*
A. A professor recognized my ambition for a combined program of research and clinical work along with my severe limitations—no money and little English. She gave me $500.00 to put in the bank for emergencies and then got me some financial support by asking me to work as her research assistant. An-

other dean got me a partial scholarship. They saw me as friendly, quite willing to help in any way that I could, bright and ambitious.

Q. *Any mentors at Ohio University?*
A. During my masters program, my major advisor was superb. He always included me in meetings with visiting psychologists and through them got me offers to stay in the United States to continue with my doctoral work. I couldn't have done that without such support.

Q. *What had you done to be noticed all along besides being smart?*
A. I was a social catalyst. I had parties and cemented friendships. I think I also was the connector between faculty and students. I was also vitally interested in their research.

Q. *Was your thesis helpful?*
A. It was too large, too ambitious for a master's thesis. The scope was unnecessary, but it provided me not only with great discipline but a real way to present my work so that the profession could be impressed with me. That advisor was instrumental in telling me where to apply for the doctoral program and what to study. I had thought I'd be returning to Greece and therefore needed a counseling rather than a clinical psychology emphasis. He saw to it I had both, so that I had the option to stay here too. As I recall, I applied to many programs, but Maryland sent me the warmest letter of acceptance.

Q. *Did you continue to get financial help at Maryland?*
A. I was offered a half-assistantship, but that wasn't enough. So immediately I went to the chair of the

department for more. In fact, he gave me total support—tuition and money in return for more teaching, research, and counseling on my part.

Q. *Any significant mentors in your doctoral program?*
A. The most difficult statistics professor gave me the greatest intellectual boost. Also, my advisor, a superb man who devoted his life to students, helped me by giving intellectual support and encouragement. He and I stayed in touch until his death. Another faculty member adopted me as a young sister. All of them included me in professional connections and faculty meetings. So, early on, I met numbers of the great people in psychology. You must remember that then Maryland was only a small department with thirty-two graduate students. I was only the second woman to get a Ph.D. in that program. I recall that when I married a classmate, the whole department held a huge wedding celebration. That sense of family continues to this day.

Jim Bellows

Executive Producer, *Entertainment Tonight*; former
editor of the *Los Angeles Herald Examiner*, *New York
Herald Tribune*, and the *Washington Star*. *Kenyon
College*, B.A., 1947, L.H.D. (honorary degree), 1965
Trustee, Kenyon College

Q. *Were you active in any extracurricular activities
in college, such as a fraternity?*
A. In fact, I was the president of my fraternity.

Q. *Did you have an outside job or something like an
internship at Kenyon?*
A. Not one that you would normally think of. Of
course I worked summers in a gas station and box-
packing factory. But I went to college during World
War II and had to take a three-year intervention
with the United States Navy as a pilot. When I flew
solo, I felt very philosophical for the first time. I
understood only then that to live well you have to
be involved and that you have to have passion. When
I came back to college from the war, I realized that

140

there was not enough student participation. I began to change that by rewriting the student constitution.

Q. *Did you want something different for yourself as a result of the Navy?*
A. Yes. I also changed my career goal. Before the Navy, I had wanted to be either a purser on the Grace Line or a stockbroker—something to do with accounts. But when I came back, I was much more reflective. I recall my father asking me about my goals. He was eager to help connect me, and he sent me around to numbers of his friends. I rejected the idea of nepotism and turned down their offers. After all, it was my professor of philosophy who became a mentor to me and helped me direct my course.

Q. *How did that happen?*
A. When I was unsure, so unsure, I went to see him and told him I was thinking of being a stockbroker so I could make a lot of money. His response was to tell me to figure out a way of life and a reason for life. Then he suggested newspapers. He had always wanted that for himself and had tried in Cincinnati but had not been successful. He thought I might be. So I put an ad in a trade paper and took my first full-time job in a newspaper in Georgia. And that was the beginning.

Comment: Mentors, like everyone else, are often forced to choose one field of study over another and then find themselves keenly interested in still another field, which they do not have time to pursue. Their protégés, particularly undecided ones, may pick up their challenge and make it their own.

Jay Bernstein

Talent Manager of Suzanne Sommers, Farrah
Fawcett, and other stars.
Pomona College, California, B.A., History, 1959

Q. *Were you active in extracurricular activities?*
A. I had to be. I came from an Episcopal Preparatory
School in the south with only twenty-two classmates.
I had to learn how to talk to a variety of people.
There were no fraternities permitted during the first
year, so I started one with eleven members. Then in
the second year, I joined a real fraternity and became
the vice president and social chair. I planned theme
parties with great imagination—caves, etc. I had to
learn how to be flashy. I figured college had to be
my halfway house between high school and life. I
was never a great student, so I learned what I needed
to know—how to figure the angles and make something creative happen. I could never have learned
this on my own. I needed a rich, well-centered place

like Pomona, and rich, well-connected students who were curious. It was the training group that I needed. I do the same thing now as a business.

Q. *Did you have any mentors?*
A. There was only one professor who understood me, Richard Armour. He taught a class in creative writing at Scripps, one of the sister colleges in the Claremont system. I was the only one to sign up and therefore got to know him.

Kathleen Connell

Vice President of Chemical Bank, Director of
Financial Consulting in Housing Finance;
community activist serving on the boards of the
Venice Free Clinic, The Public Inebriate Program,
Assaults Against Women, Women in Business,
and UCLA Dean's Council.
Hastings College, B.A., Political Science, 1965–69
American University, B.A., Political Science, 1968–69
University of Pittsburgh, Regional Economics M.A.,
HUD Fellowship, 1972–74
UCLA, Ph.D., Finance study

Q. *Were you active in extracurricular activities?*
A. Oh, absolutely. I was a class officer, student body
officer, president of my co-ed dormitory, chair of the
Campus Judicial Board, vice president of the Inter-
sorority Council, and an editor of the newspaper.

Q. *Was there any professor who was significant in
helping you to develop?*
A. Yes, one, in fact, in my freshman year revolu-
tionized my life. I became a real student only because
of his aggressive insistence that I work harder than
I thought I could. He felt my approach to college was
that of a dilettante and was determined to make a
scholar of me. He succeeded—I graduated with honors and won a full scholarship for graduate study.

Q. *Did you use any paper or thesis to help you launch into what you thought you might like to do?*

A. Yes, in a special program at American University, I wrote a major thesis on the decision processes by which the content of evening news shows is silenced. I had initially written to NBC asking for an internship, and when they responded asking me to analyze this issue, I eagerly agreed. The opportunity to observe the internal workings of a national network and to meet the "name" newscasters, including John Chancellor and Chet Huntley, was an extraordinary experience for me. A specific research topic provided the access to much broader operations.

In a second instance, I was writing a thesis for a master's program as a HUD Fellow. My topic was New Towns' Development and exposed me to the actual local environments of several large-scale developments and major builders. So when my thesis was published, my reputation was established.

Later, I returned to UCLA as a research assistant to Harvey Perloff, chair of the Architecture and the Urban Planning Department, who became a mentor to me. Through his continuous and generous influence and special instructions to the political and business communities, I applied for the job that I now have.

Lee Elman

Q. *Were you involved in leadership roles in any extracurricular activities?*

A. I was the manager of the Triangle Club, the Princeton variety show, and arranged for a seventeen-city tour. I was also the manager of the tennis team. Then I helped organize the debate team while I learned how to present my ideas and facts and collect my thoughts. I debated Kissinger in 1957, I recall.

Q. *How did you hear of the Woodrow Wilson School of International Affairs?*

A. I saw the notice posted and entered; only fifty of us of the 750 won. During the summers of my second and third years I prepared my thesis in Rome, which in turn prepared my way for the Fulbright.

Q. *Did you have any mentors?*
A. Several in different fields, but Mme. Oppenheim was the most significant. She had a salon in the great European tradition and exposed me to the most wonderful and talented people. She also helped me overcome stuttering. She was a true mentor for a long time, and I am grateful to her for so much.

Q. *Did you continue these involvements in law school?*
A. Yes, and I specifically chose Yale because it offered a broad-spectrum approach to law nearly interdisciplinary. I specialized in international law and was president of the World Communities Association.

Q. *Did you take an internship in law school?*
A. During my second year I went to Paris to intern without pay with an American law firm. I paid for it by simultaneously getting a Mobil grant. I worked two months for Mobil and two months for the law firm. I remember that I had to get special dispensation to come back to Yale late. That was how I got to write the two-volume study of practical issues for multinational operations which was so critical to my own career.

Q. *Any influential professors?*
A. A number of professors important to me were specialists in the arts and philosophy — architecture, Italian, French literature, and ethics — as well as law and international business.

Q. *Did you work after your internship?*
A. In fact, by my last year, I had formed my first business, an international investment company.

Frank Gehry

Architect, F.A.I.A; the Charlotte Davenport Professor
of Architecture at Yale University; winner of
numerous A.I.A. awards.
University of Southern California, Bachelor of
Architecture, 1949–54
Harvard, Planning, 1956–57

Q. *Were you particularly influenced by any professors?*

A. I graduated from high school thinking I would
be a chemical engineer like my cousin. But I started
at USC as a fine arts major and worked with a professor developing glaze fittings. Its chemistry suited
me and I worked ravenously, going the extra mile.
It was he who encouraged me to consider architecture, sensing that I "sparkled" around its ideas. I,
myself, had never even thought of architecture. He
must have pulled some strings and got me into the
night class, just to try it out. Of course it worked,
and for the first time I was a great student, not an
average one, and was skipped into the second year.
I sought out two or three professors with liberal po-

litical views which matched mine and hung out with them. I only know now how much paying inordinate attention and giving complete support counts. Only then could I be included in everything from working on projects to dinners at their houses while most of the other students were into fraternities.

Q. *Did you work during college?*
A. I got a job with Gruen, then the most idealistic firm, combining business with planning for all the right causes. I got the job, as I now recall, through the dean's intervention. He simply called Victor Gruen and asked him to take me.

Q. *Why would the dean have done that for a student?*
A. I had known him well. I had dropped into his office, and there we had had long discussions, particularly about politics, the need to declare oneself versus sitting on the fence. We didn't agree, but we talked and came to know each other.

Q. *Did you use your architectural thesis to your advantage?*
A. I was one of the few who got paid to do the thesis and got to be known in the process. I had a Mexican student friend who had a job large enough to get my professors involved in what became a development project for a whole Mexican town. I started off moonlighting, but then it turned out that several of us each used a piece of the project as our theses.

Q. *How did you choose Harvard's Planning School?*
A. Back in the fifties, planning rather than architecture was the liberal ideal. One of my professors at USC had taken me under his wing. He had coauthored an urban planning text with the dean of USC and recommended me. Once there, after the

army, I found that my classes were all statistics and government. I knew I couldn't excel in that program, and I needed to come back to architecture. I left after one year when a scout from Pereira's architectural firm found me.

I am now teaching at the Yale Architecture School and realize that my students inspire me. We become a two-way support system, which usually survives the school period.

Mollie Gregory

Screenwriter; author; president of Women in Film.
New York University Film School, B.A., 1965,
M.A., 1966

Q. *How important was college in your life?*
A. In some ways, I *am* my college career. I battled for a year and a half to be a film or TV directing major, but got shunted into writing. Discrimination against women as directors at the time was quite powerful—as it still is. Their reason then was, of course, that the cameras were too heavy for us to lift.

Q. *Did you work while you were in college?*
A. I did not have the most financially advantaged background. For the first two years I worked full-time as a secretary to a physician so I could go to school at night. I would not recommend that course unless absolutely necessary.

Q. *Did you have any mentor or professor who was willing to help you in any way?*

A. Several significant people helped me enormously. One was the chair of the department who told me that the department offered the MCA script award for two thousand dollars. Winning that award did wonderful things for my ego and made it possible for me to go to school during the day, which was essential. From then on, that chairperson saw to it that I knew about different awards; so I competed and won four national awards for radio and television. My professor-mentor also helped me attain an independent scholarship for graduate study to make my schooling possible. He influenced my career and we remain friends to this day.

Q. *Were there such things as internships at that time in film school?*

A. Yes, again, this professor made it possible for me to have an internship through the department. I wrote screenplays for independent producers and eked out an existence for myself to support my full-time study.

As a matter of fact, out of all these and subsequent production experiences of making my way in the field, I wrote *Making Films Your Business* (Schocken Books, New York, 1980) to help others find theirs.

Amy Kopelan

Director of Early Morning Programming, ABC-TV.
Boston University, B.S., 1973
School of Public Communication

Q. *Were you involved in extracurricular activities?*
A. I did everything that I could in college. During my first year, I was involved in dormitory activities, on the food and housing committees and student government projects. In my second year, I was the head of that food and housing committee. I had to campaign for the position and found it as exciting as it had been running for class president for three years in high school.

Q. *Why did you choose the food and housing committee of all committees?*

A. It instantly gave me a liaison role between the students and the adults professionally involved both on campus and outside.

Q. *Were you noticed by your university?*
A. In my third year, I was one of the fifteen selected by the alumni committee to join the group called the President's Hosts, representing the university at social events. Then in my fourth year, I was selected to be the chair of the President's Hosts after extensive recommendations and a series of interviews. It was quite an honor for me. At the same time I volunteered to be the chair of the Student Course Evaluation Book for my school, Public Communications. And at the end of my senior year, I was one of the few to receive the Cap and Crown Award, a special award chosen by previous members of Cap and Crown and school faculty and administration. My long list of activities suddenly made me aware how much I had done and had learned.

Q. *What did you learn from all this extensive activity?*
A. Two things. First, I loved being in charge of a project, working with others and following through. I find I'm really uncomfortable when I don't have my hand in and when I'm not in control. Secondly, I learned how to delegate tasks, because I couldn't do everything myself. Therefore I had to learn who to choose to do which tasks, a critical lesson, I must say.

Q. *Did you use these same techniques of intense involvement to get a job while you were in college?*
A. In fact, I did, at the end of my junior year. I knew

you had to have contacts, so I set about asking everyone I knew, including my parents. My father knew a maintenance engineer at ABC and asked him to give him the name of someone I might talk to. That was the Director of New Operations, who explained production work, showed me how videotaping worked, introduced me to the engineers, and told me to come back after graduation. As it turned out, one of the engineering supervisors suggested that I train right then for the summer, which meant taking the midnight to eight A.M. shift. I did, was hired, and then I was switched to day and then switched again.

A year later, just before graduation, I got a tip call from a friend telling me that ABC was again hiring for temporary jobs. I called and got permission to leave school early to take the job. I moved in with my aunt in New York, took a week off to graduate, and then was back to work the day afterward. The job was to last until September, but I was asked to stay. Then there was a three-month layover from December until March. I gambled that they would ask me back, and in April they did. Here I am, six years later.

Q. *Was there any professor who acted as a mentor to you in college?*
A. There were two. One was the most demanding, exacting professor, who made us think specifically about television production. His assignments were to do completely full programs which superseded the "exercise" level of most classes. I learned to organize and schedule all with the best effort always and without direct supervision. I am grateful to him. My advisor helped me on a more personal level. She was compassionate and supportive, acting more like a

therapist might. She encouraged me, telling me I was heading exactly in the right direction; she helped me build self-confidence.

Burt Metcalfe

Producer of the "M*A*S*H" television series.
*University of California, Los Angeles, Theater Arts
Department*, B.A., Drama, 1955

Q. *Were you involved in extracurricular activities in college?*
A. Ironic though it now seems, my first impulse was to be an actor; therefore, I was active in theater arts. I began acting in my freshman year. College was a happy and successful world for me, and I was appointed president of the theatrical drama society, Kap and Bells. Basically I was not a joiner nor an aspirant of positions of power, so this was the first time I was recognized as a leader and trusted. It was very fulfilling.

Q. *Did any professors encourage you?*
A. My professors encouraged me on an extracurricular level, but academically they discouraged act-

ng just as they discouraged it for everybody. The purpose at UCLA was to train educators and others, not actors. I tried to get myself a well-rounded education, not a trade acting background. And I must say, my professors were right; the larger framework taught me to have an awareness to understand and appreciate. The fact that people trusted me was the greatest attribute of all.

Q. *What was your first job?*

A. I got my first job in casting. It is only in hindsight that I realize how much UCLA has helped me. I realized how much I knew about acting and the theater, how much taste and knowledge I had acquired.

Q. *How did you get to direct "M*A*S*H"?*

A. In the fourth season the producers encouraged me to take the plunge. Directing provided a rush for me, a high and exciting desire to help other actors. I had given up acting as a way to manifest love and made some new decisions about my life. It was through my casting experience that Twentieth Century Fox hired me to cast two pilots. One was "M*A*S*H" and the other was "Anna and the King of Siam." "Anna" lasted thirteen weeks, but here we are on "M*A*S*H" eleven years later. As I think about it, my main characteristics have not been tremendously aggressive or greatly striving. Much of what has happened to me has also been a matter of being in the right place at the right time and being able to respond to opportunity.

Carolyn See

Professor of English at Loyola Marymount
University; novelist, magazine writer, and book
reviewer, the *Los Angeles Times*.
Los Angeles City College, A.A., 1953
Los Angeles State College, B.A., 1955
University of California, Los Angeles, M.A., 1959 and
Ph.D., 1963

Q. *How important was your college life to you?*
A. It was my only real home, the main staple in my life. I started from the lowest rung in the most dire financial straits. When I went to Los Angeles City College, I was kicked out of my own home after high school graduation and I lived in a rented room. I supported myself by being a waitress for seventy-five cents an hour. The idea then was that nothing bad can ever happen to you, that you can always make it. That's how I lived my life. I continued waitressing through Los Angeles State College. Waitressing isn't a bad job. It provided great exercise, change in your pocket, and food to eat. It's not bad for an upwardly mobile, bright, perky student.

Q. *Was graduate school different?*

A. Well, I got in. One nice professor wrote a strong letter of recommendation for me. I stayed in graduate school, I think, for emotional security. It became a place to come to meet friends. It was the best of times. I loved every aspect of it. Nobody ever said anything to me about a career. I remember that we made movies, played charades, had picnics. It was everything that home should be. I know that school should give students that kind of support system; to give stability while allowing students to try out what they want.

Q. *Was there a mentor or a specific professor who acted as a mentor to you?*

A. Yes, indeed. John Espey was the best, most scholarly professor and the funniest, a wonderful combination. I remember that our small Modern American Literature seminars left me helpless with laughter. I remember switching to Espey after having worked for somebody else. In fact, I was terrified of him and was his first doctoral candidate. He arranged for me to be a teaching assistant in the English department and made it possible for me to compete for the Woodrow Wilson Teaching Fellowship. Then he saw to it that I had a career by making it possible for me to get a two-year instructorship until my husband graduated.

Q. *As a professor, do you find yourself doing any of those things that your mentor did for you?*

A. Yes, of course. However, in the beginning I did more for students and encouraged more of them to talk to me than I do now. As I write more seriously, I want to test my students first, giving them several things to do before I provide warm comfort. But I help them get jobs and assignments. I'm happy to do that. That's what all writers should do for each other.

Lesley Stahl

CBS White House Correspondent.
Wheaton College for Women, B.A., Liberal Arts and
European History, 1963

Q. *Did you know what you wanted to study when you started at Wheaton?*
A. No, not at all. My tests showed that my strongest aptitude was in science, which was exactly what my teachers—it was the Eisenhower years—were encouraging. But I really wanted to study history. It wasn't my strong suit... actually it was my weak one... but I was determined even though my Professors argued against it. I recall also that I didn't use history in my career; I didn't know then what my career would be! Journalists, I have come to find out, have personalities that like to stand on the side and watch rather than be in the middle of things. That suits me exactly, but I didn't know it then and didn't have any direct experience to discover it.

Q. *Was there a benefit to being at a women's college?*
A. Absolutely. First of all, we had male professors and were trained to argue with men. But even more important, there was an attitude that women could do anything—and should. There was no hint in my education that women could not run things... or rise to the top. It came as a shock on my first job when someone said, "They never promote women here." This was an alien concept and I quit. I believe in women's colleges strongly and am an active alumnae, serving on Wheaton's Board.

Q. *Did you take advantage of writing a thesis to help your career?*
A. I wrote a long thesis on how World War II actually started. I was trying to isolate what "force" was the most determining one. I found it wasn't economics, but the human factor—a question of political incompetence. I remember that my advisor was tremendously helpful. I didn't write the thesis though, with career in mind. I was just interested in the subject for its own sake.

Q. *Did you go on to graduate school as a matter of course?*
A. I went to Columbia University and floundered there for another year and a half, trying for science and medicine. I still did not trust myself, you see. Then I left to take my first job with the Population Council. That is the group I left as soon as I saw how women were treated.

Q. *How did you discover journalism and news reporting after all this?*
A. I was so frustrated that I answered an ad in *The New York Times* for a researcher for John Lindsay's

speech-writing staff. The moment I saw a press office up close, a light bulb went off in my head. Truly, it was an internal explosion. The idea of reporting had never presented itself before—but there it was. I had never written for my college newspaper, you see; I certainly wished I had. It might have saved a lot of time.

Gloria Steinem

Editor of *Ms.* magazine.
Smith College, B.A., 1956

Q. *Were you involved in any extracurricular activities?*
A. I did some insignificant writing for the paper — book reviews and that sort of thing. But nothing important.

Q. *Did you have any internship or work?*
A. I was a moderately poor kid in a rich school. I worked summers, but was able to take my junior year abroad. But looking back, I didn't use it well at all.

Q. *Did you have any mentors?*
A. One professor who taught the history of India took an interest in me. When I was graduating, I was faced with two dead-end jobs: researching for

Time-Life, which had never let women actually write at that time, and being engaged to marry. Instead, my professor encouraged me to go to India on an experimental fellowship. At first it provided me a necessary escape from that job and marriage, two socially enormous pressures. But then I discovered so much more and was awakened politically. I had received the first of three fellowships given for India and wrote the guide for the subsequent groups.

I was really alone, one of two Westerners actually living at the University of Delhi. Their classes were then poor quality, left over from the English colonial days. But I met so many people and went to stay with a woman, a junior "Emma Goldman," who had been married to a prominent Indian communist. I also travelled with a Ghandian. We witnessed the terrible caste riots in villages. I discovered for the first time real poverty and politics. We Americans were certainly not the norm; we were like a cupcake in the midst of a starving world. I was more at home there in India than I was in Europe during that junior year abroad. India was welcoming and diverse. It was, now that I think of it, the beginning of my political life.

When I came home to the states in 1958, nobody was interested in India. It was too early. I lived on sofas of friends for three months before I found a job. Few people were interested in student politics in those post-McCarthy days—not my friends nor any employers. My first job came through an American who had been interested in international student politics. Then I became a freelance writer.

After these twenty-four years, it is a major revelation to me now that I am finally happy just where I am—at *Ms.* magazine here in New York.

Cynthia Tivers

Producer of "P.M. MAGAZINE".
Northwestern University, B.A., Journalism, 1969

Q. *What was the most important aspect of college for you?*
A. I had an open mind to a lot of information, and my advisor was helpful to me in choosing what courses I should take. Since I was married, my time outside school was divided between home and work. I always worked as a reporter, a stringer for community papers, covering an election for a network. The most important part always was working at anything related to my field.

Q. *Did you have a paid job?*
A. I was paid for my work as a free-lance reporter for a community paper in Chicago. I covered school board and village meetings. Reporting enabled me

to practice what I was learning in journalism classes. And I must say, earning money for my work made me feel important.

Q. *Did you also participate in any internships?*
A. Journalism school did not have any established internships, but the speech department did. I knew I needed contacts for a job, and I knew that any internship would help. So, I talked the speech department advisor into letting me in. In my last quarter, the summer session, I spent some time at each of the three Chicago television stations: WGN, WTTV, and WMAQ. Then I took a receptionist's job with WMAQ and tried hard to make a place for myself writing and reporting amid answering the phones. One radio reporter there was very encouraging, and when a sufficient amount of time went by without new openings on permanent staff, he referred me to the editor of a suburban chain of daily papers who hired me for my second full-time job.

Taking chances and making contacts counts.

Art Ulene

The "Feeling Fine" physician; author; television medical expert for *The Today Show*, ABC News. *University of California at Los Angeles*, B.S., M.D.

Q. *Were you involved in extracurricular activities?*
A. I belonged to a fraternity that was important to me; however, I was premed and I had blinders on in order to get into medical school, my first priority. My second priority was making sure that I could support myself in school for undergraduate and then for medical school.

Q. *Did you have a job to support yourself through?*
A. Yes, indeed, I worked as an entrepreneur. I ran a day camp business started by two friends. Our intent was not only to support ourselves very well but to have the best day camp around. We ran the camp so successfully that we started another and had the two camps compete against each other. I learned

an enormous amount about business and became a good financial manager. For example, I learned to get others to invest in the future of the camp. Principally, I learned how to harness my energy, to be honest, to create excitement through it all. That's all you've got unless you have a rich father.

I wish that there had been more time to study more subjects, for example, but there wasn't. The day camp, by the way, ran for seven years and then the three of us sold it for a large profit. It financed undergraduate and medical school education for the three of us. It still exists; my daughter, in fact, has applied for a job there.

Q. *Were there any professors who became mentorlike to you?*
A. I had two or three excellent professors whom I admired very much, but the classes were too large. After a second year in medical school I did receive a cancer fellowship that was given only to two people based on both competence and interest. I had a double attention for science, particularly pathology, and for business. I see now that that all comes together in the books that I write on health, and my appearances on local and national news shows as the "Feeling Fine" physician, and in my latest venture, the Cable Health Network.

Ted Williams

Chairman and Chief Executive Officer,
Bell Industries (conglomerate,
New York Stock Exchange).
University of Michigan, B.S., 1942
Mechanical and Industrial Engineer

Q. *Was college an important part of your life?*
A. Going to college was the most formative time, both socially and in my career. It was my total life, then, my whole existence. I lived on campus in rooming houses. I worked for professors in the engineering department, taught, and developed mentors. Even now my two closest classmates are my associates.

Q. *Did you work in addition to a teaching assistantship?*
A. I worked summers in a tool and die shop, which became the most helpful to me for manufacturing.

Q. *Did you think of an academic career yourself?*
A. Yes, I went to graduate school in 1942 and taught

ordinance inspectors at the same time. Then I had to go into the army. When I came back I was advised not to teach, since I would have to give up the use of my management talent in industry.

Amnon Yariv

Professor of Electrical Engineering and Applied
Physics; Thomas G. Myers Chair, California Institute
of Technology.
University of California, Berkeley, B.S., 1951,
Ph.D., 1959

Q. *Did any professor who was important to you help
you in undergraduate work?*
A. You must understand that I was largely apolit-
ical then. I was interested mainly in the intellectual
side of studies. My drive to understand the material
more deeply than the class level caused me often to
stay after classes and talk to the teachers. In this
manner I got to know some of the professors quite
closely even as an undergraduate and vice versa.

Q. *Did you use any papers or a thesis to your advantage?*
A. I published as a graduate student, but that was
not very unusual. Some of us were "partners" with
our professors in science.

Q. *How did you choose the laser field? Was it your specific interest at the beginning of graduate school?*
A. Absolutely not. I had started to do something else altogether. But at a meeting I heard about a new invention, lasers, which opened an entirely new field. I went to visit the inventor at his laboratory (Bell Labs), and he helped me enormously technically, then recruited me after I graduated. I went to work at the same place, I might add, and stayed there for five years. I also remained excellent friends with my major professor. They are, in fact, some of my best personal friends and enjoy working in similar fields.

Q. *How risky is it to choose a completely new field as your dissertation subject?*
A. It was high risk for me to have chosen the ambitious thesis in the area of quantum electronics, which includes lasers. It was the first such project at the University of California in Berkeley. The risk lay in my not having any experts to help me. But at the same time the success of the project and the resulting publications had brought me to the attention of the leading U.S. scientists working in the field while I was still a student. So I was offered a job at the Bell Telephone Laboratories before I even left Berkeley.

Q. *Did you also have a job during your undergraduate and graduate days?*
A. Yes, I worked as an undergraduate during the year doing every imaginable job from construction to short-order cooking in a boys' rooming house to chauffeuring old ladies. During the summers I had the perfect seasonal job because it paid well for a student—I drove a forklift for a cannery for three

summers. None of these jobs meant anything; they just afforded my way. I also had a tuition scholarship, which helped me as a foreigner; the tuition was quite steep.

Appendix:

Experts Talk About the Latest Developments in College Career-Planning Services

Nearly every college and university now has a department or center devoted to career planning and development. I have talked to dozens of directors of these centers, in large and small institutions, general and specialized, and asked what services they offer and what career advice they would give to today's students. What follows in this chapter is a summary of some of these discussions to help acquaint you with what is happening in the career development field on campuses today.

As a private career consultant, I have found time and time again that people will not ask for help until they are stuck. It is the same with students. Most college career directors report that their toughest task is to persuade students to take advantage of their centers early and not wait until the final three months of their last year to descend upon a counselor. Therefore, as bait, career planners offer what they think students want first—vocational testing and resume-writing workshops.

Dr. Christopher Shinkman, Director of the Career Planning and Placement Center at Stanford University in Palo Alto, California, and author of *Career Development in the 1980s: Theory and Practice* (Charles Thomas, 1981), conducts workshops during freshman orientation week in which counselors explain key career service offerings aimed particularly at underclassmen. Director Thomas Bachhuber of the University of Maryland's Career Development Center and author of *Directions: A Guide for Career Planning* (Houghton Mifflin, 1977), similarly uses freshmen orientation week for his media presentation, with the goal of introducing students to the college career planning process by showing them successful student role models. Through another program for new students, Bachhuber uses an experimental display to point out the relationship among career goals, requisite skills, academic courses and extracurricular choices.

Director Celestine Schall at Alverno College's Career Development and Placement Center has assessment tapes available for the all-female student body. Each year every student is videotaped talking about her interests and goals. She may then not only witness her own growth in communication skills, but her changing interests as well. At the senior level, simulated job interviews are also included on the tape. This remarkable system, so inexpensive, so revealing, can easily be instituted in every center.

Ms. Schall has also pioneered the Off-Campus Experiential Learning Concept—OCEL. With full administrative support, Alverno has institutionalized the process of making what is learned in class apply outside the classroom. Faculty are included in helping students to bridge their disciplines with possible careers. For example, with the aid of the academic advisor, English majors must declare a direction within their study, such as journalism, research, teaching, or personnel management. Then the faculty and the career center work together to provide plans and actually broker such interest in the business community. The faculty are responsible for going out to survey people working in the arts, business, medical, and public service communities to find out what people actually do on their jobs and what skills and interests best suit those tasks. The Faculty Institute then works together with the Career Development Office to develop plans and courses that link academic study with career opportunity. OCEL provides direction and academic credit as a regular part of the student's major requirements.

Exposing students to the outside demythologizes them from media stereotypes regarding work and working. The old European ideal of the ivory tower notion of universities is antiquated. Students need to be out watching people by getting involved with them in any way possible, according to Howard Figler at the University of Texas at Austin's Career Center. Developing a system of mentors for students in formal or not-so-formal ways is a growing phenomenon in most colleges. Good candidates to become mentors are alumni active in diverse careers. For the most part, they can be asked to volunteer their time for anything from a brief interview in which they explain what they do and offer advice on entry to the profession, to their actually helping set up jobs and internships.

Barbara Lazarus, Director of Wellesley's Center for Women's Careers, believes that alumnae can be used as coaches. Wellesley has developed an internship program that it considers essential. And students are encouraged to participate throughout their undergraduate program. Although usually no credit is received, this field experience is taken advantage of by at least one third of the student population.

At the University of Maryland, Director Thomas Bachhuber has also developed an extensive alumni network, one in which they return to tell first-hand about their work in a career decision-making course.

At Stanford University, Director Christopher Shinkman urges students to take advantage of internships in government as well as hospitals, law firms, and private industry near campus. Alumni are willing to serve as active career counselors in order to build the internship program of their alma mater. At this particular college, faculty sponsors determine whether internships earn academic credits.

At the University of Virginia, Director Larry Simpson reports that forty percent of alumni is actively involved in the internship process. For example, a third-year speech and communications major was matched with the president of a major film company through an executive of a parent corporation. The executive, of course, was an alum. Another student, interested in sports writing, was given the chance to interview with the Baseball Commissions Office.

Judith Katz, former Director of the Swarthmore Career Center, instituted a program of externships, in which students "shadow" a professional, usually an alumni, for a certain period of time in order to get a feel of what work in that profession is like. Influenced by the Swarthmore program, the University of Virginia has begun its own externship program. More than five hundred students spend one full week matched with participating alumni. Students must compete for this valuable experience.

A career is comprised of "human events, not sociological categories," comments Dr. Robert Ginn, Director of Personnel Management, Faculty of Arts and Sciences at Harvard. To determine what you want to start with, begin by watching people work. Connections with alumni are vital and are used to set up many visits and more than two hundred internships.

Director Robert Ehrmann of UCLA's Placement and Career Planning Center reports that some internships serve as prerequisites to industries where entry is otherwise difficult. Advertising and public relations in Los Angeles, for example, practically demand internships or similar connections as a way of breaking in.

With all the workshops and programs set up to help students find out who's who and what's what in the career business, the question that still haunts most students is how to decide what to do in the first place. This is by far the toughest question they face. Many of us, especially during our student days, tend to think of work in abstract ways. "I want to work with people" is a phrase I hear constantly in my own consulting practice, and one that must be reframed and made more specific. Career directors in colleges and universities across the country scan such an abstraction in various ways.

Dr. Howard Figler at the University of Texas at Austin:

> Students must find meaning from their experiences. And their experiences come from activities, jobs, internships, which is where they develop both skills and priorities. Therein lie all the clues. For example, if the student has a part-time job working in food service, you go with that. The student typically believes that the work has been meaningless. But you could get him to consider what his experience actually meant. He might have supervised others, dealt with negotiating and haggling, created inventories or food ideas.

Director James Briggs of the Career Planning and Placement Center at the University of California at Berkeley:

> You take students beyond the original abstraction by having them get a job and thereby get experience. They need to start with even the experience of talking to working people about what they do. Then you essentially go back to fundamental steps and work students backward to a skill-identification process. That way you link a student with interests and values to find a purpose. I use Crystal's approach, and instead of getting at occupational titles, you go after statements of desired future accomplishments. You move a student from saying, "I want to be an environmentalist," to "I want to im-

prove the environment." Then you can proceed by asking what some options are for doing that: writing, fund raising, politics, or working directly with governmental groups. What we should do is not get students only to get first jobs, but to teach the process of making decisions about what to do.

Director Celestine Schall of the Career Development and Placement Center at Alverno College, Milwaukee:

We teach a process to find appropriate positions and then use our contacts. We first ask more specific questions and keep narrowing the field to provide examples. When do you like working with people? What kind of people? In what ways? Our students become skilled, then, in being specific about what they might like to try first. Later we ask them to attempt an oral job description to a potential employer in a simulated interview tape and replay. That procedure helps focus them more on their abilities and potential contributions.

Dr. Thomas Bachhuber, Director of the Career Development Center at the University of Maryland:

We must help students destroy the myth that a career choice will just come to them as part of college. Successful choices happen only if they take advantage of resources, programs and people that are there to help in college. Our career library, for example, has the *Guide to Occupational Exploration* and the *Dictionary of Occupational Titles*, which I like to have students use as ways to picture themselves in various functions and tasks described.

Dr. Larry Simpson, Director of the Career Planning and Placement Office at the University of Virginia:

> The best way to deal with the "I want to help people" syndrome is directly through our career resource network. We contact about five hundred people for students to get to talk with. These sessions are brief, an hour and a half, and occur no more than once a month. By talking to practitioners in plants, factories, and businesses, students get to focus, narrow, and redefine what they want. We encourage students, once they have done this, to develop the habit of talking to others. We help by providing a list of typical questions they might start with.

Director Pat Rose of Career Planning and Placement at the University of Pennsylvania:

> We question students to determine specifically what they already do well, what kinds and how many people do they want to work with, under what circumstances. Then we also provide workshops and individual counsel. Each of our eleven staff members has a single constituency like Wharton, or the College of the Arts and Sciences.

Robert Erhmann, Director of Career Development at UCLA, confirms the importance of questions:

> In the lack of all other evidence, we will usually go with what students feel they do their best work in and the areas that they have had longstanding and consistent interest patterns in. The statement, "I want to work with people," I

believe is a fair one, but is so nonspecific that it needs to be explored in much greater depth. Answers to questions such as: What kinds of people? What kinds of settings? What kinds of relationships?—i.e., service, information-providing, direct assistance, and how they know that about themselves—are all helpful bits of information to have when assisting students.

Director Robert Ginn of Personnel Management at Harvard University:

Firsthand exploration of the phenomenal field is the most important. But I believe that testing moves students quickly and effectively into exploration by providing some tentative hypotheses about self and the world of work.

Barbara Lazarus, Director of the Center for Women's Careers at Wellesley:

In our center we are in the process of change and redirection. We also offer more support in practicing skills along with supplying information. Traditionally, students would have been sent out on interviews. Now we might ask them to read and think about them, write up some sample questions, come back, and practice some strategies together through role plays. We've found that students really don't know what to say. We are now actively coaching, not just telling.

I believe that there will be more of a move from general information-giving and assigning students library work on the nature of work to direct strategy-making or coaching. But the task is not an easy or clear one for many reasons. First, career counselors themselves are infrequently from the business communities themselves. Secondly, students are increasingly experience-poor and need desperately to have opportunities to work and be held accountable. Third, they need these experiences in a greater variety of fields and tasks and a place to talk about them in order to know more about themselves. And fourth, there needs to be greater involvement on campus with the diversity of the city, state, even federal communities.

The reality is that most colleges and universities attract the presence of only large corporations. Only large companies can afford to hire and send recruiters. Unwittingly therefore, higher educational institutions become brokers for large corporations and often form their closest links for internships, externships, and alumni contacts.

It may be that only returning students are more likely to be interested in small businesses and entrepreneurialism. There is certainly nothing wrong with working for large corporations. But too many students rely on big business for only extrinsic rewards—high salaries, expense accounts, titles, all kinds of benefits. Rewards themselves are chosen rather than the nature of the work itself or the compatibility between an individual's goals and a company's vision. James Briggs laments that students are often so concerned about career relevance that in making career decisions they tend to latch on to extrinsic reward in a sort of supply-demand situation. This means they look for the jobs that are easiest to find and the best paying.

But how to remedy that? Howard Figler thinks that perhaps a few years off between high school and college might end the parent trap which infantalizes students. He wonders how to wean people from what I call the "entitlement factor"—choosing a job with the hope or expectation that things will automatically come one's way. He adds, the worst is to see a young person at thirty afraid to move or change because he or she is worried about losing a pension. The entitlement factor prevents students from thinking about appropriate moves for their company as well as their own entrepreneurial possibilities.

Pat Rose reminds us that fully two-thirds of our working population are employed in small businesses. It is her hope that through specific workshops or small businesses the University of Pennsylvania can redirect some more entrepreneurial students away from a big business focus. Larry Simpson, at the University of Virginia, claims rural universities have a clear advantage in this regard because small business proliferates in nonindustrial towns. His university offers undergraduate courses in entrepreneurialism. Director Christopher Shinkman confirms the big business emphasis at many college and university placement offices. Scheduling on-campus interviews with large corporations is often their most visible, best-known service. But certain misconceptions result. Students have come to believe that big business is all there is. After all, there are few public-sector, small-business, social-service, arts or nonprofit organizations which interview on campus. To meet these needs of many students, Chris Shinkman offers specific programs geared toward nonrepresented sectors: social services, the arts, government, research, entertainment, and athletics.

How to keep liberal arts students employable becomes another critical concern. Larry Simpson at

Virginia reports that one of his goals for liberal arts students is to make it possible for a philosophy major to enter banking, and a biology major to consider sales. Celestine Schall at Alverno insists that all her students declare a professional track within their major by their third year and have direct experience in that field, which usually yields a first job after graduation. In *The Complete Job Search Handbook* (Holt, Rinehart & Winston, 1979) Tom Bachhuber makes use of Howard Figler's exercises to discover transferable skills. He realizes how much effort it takes students to even recognize their skills—let alone effectively communicate them. Howard Figler himself reports that students must realize the strength of their ability to learn and give up being defensive. Students are their own worst enemies when they believe that they can't do much with a liberal arts education. The ability to learn is more powerful than the degree itself, but it often takes life experience to get students to recognize that. Figler is concerned, as are all of us, about how to get students to be better risk-takers, to get over the fear of technology, and to avoid feeling conflicted about pursuing a program aimed solely at vocational preparation.

That is just the predicament that liberal arts students find themselves in. They spend time learning how to think and at the end feel trapped by not being able to compete in the job market. Yet this feeling of entrapment exists mostly in the minds of the students.

There is so much they can do if they will only acknowledge their talents and abilities. Tom Briggs at Berkeley commented that most liberal arts students can't even begin to identify their skills and think only in terms of content skills like "programing," rather than thinking and writing. They usually lack confidence in themselves and in their education. One way to change this phenomenon is to train the faculty to help students recognize what their skills can mean. Briggs credits the strong influence of President Joel Reed of Alverno for strengthening faculty resources as well as students.

Barbara Lazarus at Wellesley continues to re-direct her efforts to use her staff and often experts—alumnae and community contacts—to provide real hands-on experiences for groups of students. Rather than only see students individually, she is mobilizing small groups so that participating students themselves can be more helpful and supportive to each other. As coaches and as counselors who historically provide printed information, tests, and inventories, her staff calls for scenarios to be worked on, strategies to be conceived, and great practice and rehearsal before venturing out.

Lazarus's model comes closest to my own. Consider the coaching analogy in sports and performing arts. In both these arenas, people want to improve, put themselves in training, and find specific coaches to help them. Traditionally no other disciplines or fields have made such direct use of experts; not sales-people, health professionals, designers, secretaries, managers, or small business owners, unless they were supervised in an initial, though typically limited, training program. Each one of us, whether new to a field or fairly well developed in it, wants to improve, contribute, share, and learn. There is nothing new about this yearning or about the process of getting it. It is essentially that of mentoring, but it is usually done outside one's organization. As a career coach in the private sector, I consider myself a paid mentor for any profession. I would say that so does every counselor in every college and university career development and planning center.

Career development is a relatively new field and has had little time to examine itself. Research is necessary to tell us what works and what does not under what circumstances for which people.

All of us expect to live through multiple careers. Consider, for example, the directors of career counseling, planning, and development centers whom I have just interviewed. Only half come from specific training in vocational education or student guidance—Larry Simpson, Christopher Shinkman, Thomas Bachhuber, Robert Erhmann. Barbara Lazarus is an anthropologist; Howard Figler is a psychologist with an M.B.A.; Patricia Rose has done extensive graduate work in literature. Three come from religious life: James Briggs was formerly a Catholic priest; Robert Ginn in his own words is "a parish priest on the weekends who does career counseling during the week;" and Celestine Schall is one of the dedicated and brilliant nuns who empower Alverno College.

Each one of us believes that work can be a special mission, a demonstrated faith, unique to each individual, ever-changing, and critical to life. Each one of us has made this version of work as a calling to our own mission. And that is as it should be.

Checklist

Throughout *Making College Pay Off*, I have suggested behaviors and attitudes to put into play in undergraduate and graduate school. Use the following summary to stimulate you to action, to spur you on when you fall into the passive-student trap, so that you *can* make opportunities for yourself.

Each checklist is organized from the simplest to the most complex activity, so that underclassmen can begin at the top and gradually work down the list as they move on to advanced courses, even graduate studies.

But success starts with small bites—learning to try, experimenting, and expanding. Only in this process does the essence of success—courage, love, and mission—have a chance to flourish. Happy ventures!

Professional Relationships/Professors and Classroom Behavior

(Lower Classmen)

- Ask questions in class;
- Sit in front and get involved in class discussions.
- Form private study groups and meet regularly; don't cram.
- Find and read professors' work.
- Make comments after class.
- Find out which professors are most respected by reading *Who's Who*, book indices, and by asking others.
- Visit professors during office hours to discuss a subject that interests you and get to know the person who teaches it.

(Upper Classmen)

- Become friendly with professors and teaching assistants.
- Find out what research or special projects are ongoing and join in on any basis, from volunteer to paid professional.

(Graduate Students)

- Establish close relationships with professors and teacher assistants who may be advocates for you later.
- Ask to attend meetings or conventions with professors, at first on an observation basis, then with some duties.

Other Professional Relationships

- Become acquainted with your advisors and the staff for student curricula (petitions, financial aid, grants, programs).
- Get to know the department staff of your declared major or one in which you have a budding interest. Every dean, for example, has a counselor, secretary, and an assistant. Introduce yourself, ask questions, and read bulletin boards for events.
- Visit the campus ombudsman, if there is one. Ask what he or she does and offer your assistance.
- Ask about independent study, exchanging one class for another, increasing your load, or taking an advanced class.

• Meet the dean of your school informally through social means and formally by attending open meetings and lectures.

Assigned Papers and Projects

- Do them early, then meet with the professor or teaching assistant to discuss the structure and concept. Or prepare a first draft and have a consultation to provide you with a framework of ideas.
- Find people who work in your chosen field and ask whether they will act as your advisors or provide you with actual case materials from their businesses.
- Compare your papers with those of other students. Form a study group. Learn how to express ideas successfully.
- Write your papers for the additional purpose of trying to publish them in a campus newspaper or magazine or in a professional journal or popular publication.

• Build on your papers, allowing each to serve as part of a whole concept that could be expanded into a thesis or dissertation.

Tests

Subjective Tests

- Compose each answer as an entire essay, with a defined beginning, middle, and end. Bring in related subjects and expand when clearly called for, not simply as filler.
- Approach your professor early with questions when topics have been given or alluded to. Show an outline of your answer to determine whether the substance and style are appropriate.
- Learn to think about what the facts mean instead of merely reciting them by rote. Learn what recognized theorists believe and state whether you agree or disagree.
- Discuss your exam afterward with your professor

to find out how you can improve your answering style or where you went wrong. Don't worry about changing your grades; concentrate on learning.

• Take notes during these sessions; it's easy to forget what is difficult to hear.

Objective Tests

• Read books on the psychology of multiple-choice tests and learn how to distinguish the patterns.
• Find old exams on file in the department, if possible, and study the questions and answers. Ask for help if necessary.

Clubs and Activities

- Find out the array of activities (such as debate, orchestra, literary journal) from the student organization office, other students, or professors. Determine which skills are required for activities that interest you.
- After you join, observe the style of the club members and try to assimilate before suggesting something new.
- Recognize the leaders and find ways to actively support them.
- Build an area of expertise within a club and commit yourself to deliver what you have promised. Specialize in one club or activity and take it to the limit.
- Experiment with different aspects and roles (supporter, leader, redirector, champion).

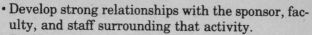

- Develop strong relationships with the sponsor, faculty, and staff surrounding that activity.
- Find business, arts, and service contacts outside the campus—all of whom might be interested in your club's activity.

Work

- Take a job that you may keep for your entire enrollment period. Realize that you can afford to do the most menial tasks at first. Once you prove your loyalty and competence, you probably can advance yourself. Don't be shy about using "connections."
- Recognize a job as a social experience and take time to meet all kinds of students and employees.
- Treat each job as if it were your own business. Think of how you would run it, in terms of management, employee motivation, customer relations, accounting, etc.
- Find existing externships or create your own, on or off campus. Discuss with others what they have done and learned from their experiences.
- Find opportunities to meet local businesspeople—

talk about your experiences and ask about theirs.
- Work as a teaching assistant to gain experience in lecturing or managing.
- Work as a research assistant in a laboratory or on a project if you are interested in developing ideas and working with a team.
- Pay as much attention to the way in which you work with people as you do in completing the task itself.

Career Counseling Services

- Go to a counseling center early and discover what it offers. Participate!
- Find out what interests you, then explore the field with assistance from the counselor.
- If you don't know what you want to do, ask for guidance and investigate several different fields.
- Take workshops and seminars to learn what professionals do, as well as to discover or confirm your interests.
- Establish a friendly relationship with career counselors. Tell them when they are helpful. Suggest other means of assistance and volunteer to arrange for it if necessary.
- Start a placement file with letters of recommendation from professors whose courses you have re-

cently taken and excelled in. It helps if you draft a letter for them, despite how difficult it is for you to do at first. Ask to see some samples from a career counselor.

- Sign up for mock interview sessions. Practice and then tape yourself. Ask others to coach you on improving your presentation.
- Use every opportunity to interview with all recruiters, even if you are not totally committed to their companies or fields.
- Be sure to contact alums in your field of interest.

About the Author

Adele Scheele, Ph.D., is a nationally known career coach. She is the author of *Skills for Success: A Guide to the Top for Men and Women* (Ballantine, March 1981) and is a syndicated columnist ("At Work") for King Features. She appears regularly on television and radio and is the work expert on "Good Morning America." Dr. Scheele often addresses colleges and universities, corporations, and professional associations. She earned a B.S. from the University of Pennsylvania, an M.A. from California State University at Northridge, and a Ph.D. from UCLA as a Change Management Fellow.

For more information about career coaching, contact Dr. Adele Scheele:

> 1722 Westwood Blvd.
> Los Angeles, CA 90024
> (213)470-2828

PLANNING YOUR CAREER
from
BEGINNING TO END...
from
Ballantine Books